Vegetarian

Nita Mehta's
SUBZIYAAN

Tasty VEGETABLES for EVERYDAY cooking

Nita Mehta's

M.Sc. (Food and Nutrition), Gold Medalist

TANYA MEHTA

SNAB
Publishers Pvt. Ltd.

Nita Mehta's SUBZIYAAN

First Edition 2002

ISBN 81-7869-031-4

Food Styling & Photography: **SNAB**

Layout and laser typesetting:

National Information Technology Academy
3A/3, Asaf Ali Road
New Delhi-110002
N.I.T.A. ☎ 3252948

Picture on cover:	*Cheesy Peppers, Dum Arbi Ratna*
Picture on page 1:	*Gajar Paneer Jalfrezi*
	Rajasthani Bharwaan Lauki
Picture on page 2:	*Cheesy Broccoli Koftas*
	Hari Gobhi- Tandoori style
Picture on last page:	*Safed Jalpari*
	Khoya Matar Makhaana
Picture on back cover:	*Stuffed Cabbage Rolls*

Published by:

SNAB Publishers Pvt Ltd
3A/3 Asaf Ali Road
New Delhi-110002

Editorial and Marketing office:
E-348, Greater Kailash-II, N.Delhi-48
Fax: 91-11-6235218 *Tel:* 91-11-6214011, 6238727
E-Mail: nitamehta@email.com
snab@snabindia.com

The Best of Cookery Books
Website: http://www.nitamehta.com
Website: http://www.snabindia.com

Printed at:
THOMSON PRESS (INDIA) LIMITED

Distributed by:
THE VARIETY BOOK DEPOT
A.V.G. Bhavan, M 3 Con Circus
New Delhi - 110 001
Tel: 3327175, 3322567; Fax: 3714335

Price: Rs.189/-

Introduction

Variety is the spice of life! Prepare your favourite vegetable in many different ways - using different spices and different combinations, thus creating totally new and delicious subzis. Cooking good food is a way of expressing your love for the family. The family gets bored and tired of eating the same style of subzi every day. They want a change! Why plan a meal outside when they desire a change. Make the day-to-day subzi tasty with just a little effort and get loads of love and hugs in return!

Vegetables make an invaluable contribution towards the **supply of minerals and vitamins and they are also low in calories**. They are rich in fibre, add bulk to the diet and assist in digestion. Every meal should include a vegetable, which may be a main dish or an accompaniment to the main dish. Delicious curries, koftas, bhujias and semi-dry masala preparations give variety to meals. **Baingan ka Saalan, Broccoli Koftas, Kachumber Gobhi, Hyderabadi Bhindi** and such many other delicacies will make your family wanting more.

The purpose of this book is to show you, how you can enjoy the same vegetable in different ways. Why think of paalak-paneer all the time! Why not - **Achaari Paalak with Corn or Paalak Mushrooms** and many more ways for any one vegetable. The book also includes *paneer and dal favourites* to accompany the subzi. Just look into your refrigerator to see what vegetable you have and go ahead with the recipe you like.

Nita Mehta

Contents

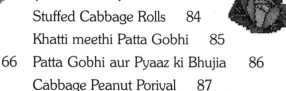

Bhein 93

Karela 97

Tinda, Parwal 101
(SMALL GOURDS)

Lauki and Turai 108
(BOTTLE GOURD & RIDGE GOURD)

Other Vegetables 113

Dal & Paneer Favourites 119

Gobhi

(CAULIFLOWER)

Phool Dilkhush

Pan fried whole cauliflowers coated with a delicious masala and topped with green peas.

Picture on facing page   *Serves 4*

2 very small whole cauliflowers

MASALA
4 tbsp oil, 3 onions - ground to a paste
3 tomatoes - roughly chopped, 1" ginger - chopped
seeds of 1 moti illaichi, 3-4 saboot kali mirch (peppercorns) and 2 laung (cloves)
2 tbsp curd - beat well till smooth
½ tsp red chilli powder, ½ tsp garam masala, ½ tsp haldi, ½ tsp amchoor
½ tsp salt, or to taste, ¼ cup boiled peas - to garnish

1. Remove stems of cauliflowers. Boil 6 cups water with 2 tsp salt. Put the whole cauliflowers in it. When the water starts to boil again, remove from fire. Leave them in hot water for 10 minutes. Remove from water and refresh in cold water. Wipe dry on a clean kitchen towel.

2. Heat 5-6 tbsp oil in a large flat kadhai or a pan. Put both cauliflowers with flower side down in oil. Cover and cook on medium flame, stirring occasionally till the cauliflowers turn golden and get patches of dark brown colour here and there. Remove from oil. Keep aside.

3. Heat ½ tbsp oil in a clean kadhai. Add moti illaichi, saboot kali mirch and laung. After a minute add chopped tomatoes and ginger. Cook for 4-5 minutes till they turn soft. Grind the cooked tomatoes to a paste.

4. Heat 3½ tbsp oil. Add onion paste. Cook till onions turn golden brown.

5. Add tomato paste. Cook for 3-4 minutes on low flame till masala turns dry.

6. Add well beaten curd. Cook till masala turns reddish again.

7. Reduce heat. Add red chilli powder, garam masala, haldi, amchoor and salt. Cook for 1 minute. Add ¼ cup water to get a thick, dry masala. Boil. Cook for 1 minute on low flame. Remove from fire.

8. Insert a little masala in between the florets of the fried cauliflower, especially from the backside.

9. To serve, arrange the cauliflowers on a platter. Add ¼ cup water to the masala to make it a masala gravy. Boil. Add ½ tsp salt or to taste. Pour over the arranged cauliflowers. Heat in a microwave or a preheated oven. Alternately, heat the cauliflower in a kadhai in 1 tbsp oil at the time of serving. Heat the masala gravy separately. Arrange the heated cauliflowers on a serving platter. Pour the hot masala gravy over it.

10. Sprinkle some boiled peas on it and on the sides. Serve.

Kathal Laajawaab : Recipe on page 115, Phool Dilkhush ➢

Gobhi Besani Tukri

Whole cauliflower, batter fried and served in the tandoori style.

Serves 4

1 small (300 gm) whole cauliflower

MARINADE
2 tbsp lemon juice
1 tsp salt
½ tsp red chilli powder
½ tsp ajwain (carom seeds)
1 tbsp ginger paste

BATTER
½ cup besan (gram flour)
¼ cup milk, approx.
1 tsp ginger paste
½ tsp ajwain
1 tbsp chopped coriander
½ tsp salt, ¼ tsp red chilli powder, ¼ tsp garam masala

SALAD
1 tomato - cut into four pieces, a few kheera slices and some onion rings

TO SPRINKLE
some chat masala

1. Remove stem of cauliflower. Boil 8 cups water with 2 tsp salt. Put the whole cauliflower in it. Put the cauliflower with stem side down. See that the whole cauliflower is dipped in water. Bring to a boil again. Boil for 3-4 minutes till the stalks turn soft. Check with a knife. Remove from fire. Remove from water and refresh in cold water. Wipe dry with a clean kitchen towel.
2. Mix all ingredients of the marinade. Insert the marinate in between the florets of the cauliflower, especially from the backside. Keep aside for 15 minutes.
3. Mix all ingredients of the batter in a deep big bowl. Add enough milk to get a thick coating batter.
4. Heat oil for deep frying in a kadhai. Dip the cauliflower in the batter. Spread the left over batter nicely with the hands on the cauliflower to cover nicely.
5. Carefully put in hot oil and deep fry till golden on medium heat. Remove from fire. Cut into four pieces. Keep aside till serving time.
6. At serving time- reheat the cauliflower pieces in a hot oven for 10 minutes or in a pan. Sprinkle chaat masala on the cauliflower and serve with salad.

Gobhi Bhare Tamatar

Tomatoes stuffed with a nutty cauliflower filling and the filling is sealed with a gramflour coating.

Serves 6-8

5 large firm tomatoes - cut into two halves

FILLING
½ of a medium cauliflower - grated
1 small boiled potato - mashed coarsely
3 tbsp oil
½ tsp jeera
¼" piece ginger - finely grated
¾ tsp salt, ¼ tsp red chilli powder
½ tsp garam masala, ¼ tsp amchoor
2 tbsp kaju (cashewnuts) - chopped
1 tbsp kishmish (raisins)
¼ tsp sugar

TOPPING
3 tbsp besan (gram flour)
a pinch of orange colour, a pinch of salt and ajwain

1. Heat 3 tbsp oil in a kadhai. Add jeera. When jeera turns golden, add ginger. Reduce heat. Saute for ½ minute. Add salt, red chilli powder, garam masala and amchoor.
2. Add cashew nuts and raisins. Stir for a few seconds.
3. Add potatoes. Cook for a minute.
4. Add grated cauliflower. Mix well. Add sugar. Cook covered for about 10 minutes, stirring frequently, till the cauliflower gets cooked.
5. Cut firm tomatoes into half. Scoop out the pulp. Rub a little salt inside and keep them upside down for 15 minutes.
6. Fill with cauliflower filling. Press well. Heat 2 tsp oil on a tawa.
7. Take out besan in a plate. Add a pinch of orange colour, salt and ajwain.
8. Holding the filling side up, invert the tomato in the besan to coat the top of the filling.
9. Invert the tomato in hot oil on the tawa with the filling side down.
10. Turn after a minute to slightly cook the other side too. Keep on fire for a short while, or the tomatoes turn limp. Turn when the side is done. Serve hot as a side dish.

Gobhi Taka-Tak

Cauliflower cooked with capsicum and tomato in masala.

Serves 4

1 medium cauliflower - cut into medium size florets with stalks
2 tbsp oil
1 tsp jeera (cumin seeds)
2 onions - chopped
1½ tbsp ginger-garlic paste
2- 4 green chillies - deseeded & chopped
¼ tsp garam masala
¼ tsp red chilli powder
1 tsp salt or to taste
2 tsp kasoori methi (dry fenugreek leaves)
½ cup dahi (yoghurt) - beat till smooth
1 tomato - cut into 8 big pieces
1 large capsicum - cut into 1" cubes

1. Break the cauliflower into medium florets, keeping the stalk intact.
2. Heat oil in a kadhai for deep frying. Add all the cauliflower pieces and fry to a light brown colour. Remove from oil and keep aside.
3. Heat 2 tbsp oil on a tawa. Add jeera.
4. When jeera turns golden, add chopped onions. Stir till onions turn transparent.
5. Add the ginger-garlic paste, green chillies, salt, chilli powder, garam masala, kasoori methi and curd. Stir-fry for 2-3 minutes till the curd dries up a little.
6. Add capsicum and tomato cubes. Fry for 1-2 minutes. Keep masala aside till serving time.
7. At the time of serving, heat the masala. Add the fried cauliflower to the masala and mix well on low heat for 2 minutes till the vegetable gets well blended with the masala. Serve hot.

Kachumber Gobhi

A dry minced preparation flavoured with fenugreek.

Serves 4-6   *Picture on page 21*

2 medium cauliflowers - cut into small florets with a little stalk
3 tbsp oil
1 tsp jeera (cumin seeds)
2" piece ginger - chopped
2 green chillies - deseeded and chopped finely
½ tsp haldi (turmeric powder)
1 tsp red chilli powder
2 tsp dhania (coriander) powder
1 tsp garam masala
2 tomatoes - chopped
2 tbsp kasoori methi (dry fenugreek leaves)
2 tbsp fresh coriander - chopped
1 tsp salt, or to taste

1. Wash and cut the cauliflower into small florets, keeping the stalk intact.
2. Heat oil in a kadhai. Add jeera and let it turn golden.
3. Reduce heat. Add chopped ginger, chopped green chillies, haldi, red chilli powder, dhania powder and garam masala. Stir fry for a minute.
4. Add chopped tomatoes and cook till oil separates.
5. Add the chopped cauliflower and a little water and stir well. Add salt to taste.
6. Cover and cook for 15-20 minutes or till the gobhi is done.
7. Add kasoori methi and stir well.
8. Serve hot sprinkled with fresh coriander.

Note: After getting cooked the gobhi becomes really kachumber. It almost gets the texture of minced gobhi.

Simla Mirch

(CAPSICUM)

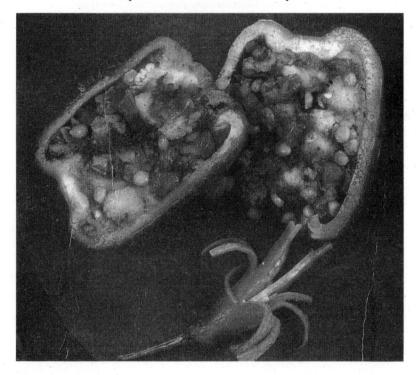

Makai Mirch

Whole Capsicums stuffed with paneer cubes mixed with mozzarella cheese and barbecued
The mozzarella cheese binds the diced paneer and corn together, as it melts on cooking.

Serves 4

4 medium size capsicums

MARINADE
2 tbsp lemon juice, 1 tsp ginger paste, ½ tsp garlic paste, 1 tbsp oil, ¾ tsp salt

STUFFING
100 gm paneer - finely cut into ¼" cubes (1 cup)
½ cup grated mozzarella cheese
½ cup corn kernels - tinned or freshly boiled
1 tbsp green coriander - chopped
2 tbsp oil
¼ tsp hing (asafoetida), 1 tsp jeera (cumin seeds)
½ tsp sarson (mustard seeds)
1 small onion - cut into half and then into rings, to get shredded onion
1 tbsp chopped cashews and 8-10 kishmish
½ tsp red chilli powder, ¾ tsp salt, ½ tsp garam masala, ¼ tsp amchoor

1. Cut a slice from the top of each capsicum. Scoop out the center with the help of a knife. Mix all the ingredients of the marinade and rub liberally on the inside of the capsicums. Cover with caps and leave aside for ½ hour.

2. For the stuffing, take a heavy bottom kadhai and heat oil. Put in the hing, jeera, and sarson. Wait till jeera turns golden.

3. Add onions and cook till soft. Add cashews and kishmish. Stir. Add red chilli powder, salt, garam masala and amchoor.

4. Add corn and coriander. Cook for 1 minute. Add paneer and mix well. Remove from fire. Add mozzarella cheese. Mix. Keep filling aside till it is no longer hot.

5. Stuff the capsicums with this filling. They should be stuffed well but not to bursting point. Rub oil on the stuffed capsicums. Cover with the caps and secure them with wooden tooth-picks.

6. Cook in a pan with 3 tbsp oil. Keep the capsicums spread out while cooking. Cook till it turns brownish- blackish from some sides. Alternately, grill in an oven by placing stuffed capsicums on the wire-rack or grill rubbed with some oil or insert on skewers. Put the skewers into the gas tandoor or oven and cook for 10 minutes or till they turn blackish at some places. Turn 1-2 times in-between to grill evenly.

Cheesy Peppers

Cheesy tomato rice stuffed in capsicums.

Picture on cover   *Serves 10*

8 green, red or yellow peppers (simla mirch)
1 tsp salt, juice of 1 lemon, 2 tsp ginger paste, 2 tbsp oil

STUFFING
2 tbsp butter
1 cup uncooked rice - soaked for 1 hour, 2 tbsp readymade tomato puree
1 onion - chopped finely
8-10 french beans - threaded and cut into small cubes
1 small carrot - cut into small cubes
100 gm mozzarella cheese - grated (1 cup), 1½ tsp salt, or to taste, ½ tsp pepper

TOPPING
4-5 tbsp grated cheese, 2 tsp tomato ketchup to dot, a few coriander or mint leaves

1. Cut a thin slice from the top of the peppers. Pull out the stalk end and make it hollow. Cut the top in a zig-zag fashion (VVVV) with a sharp kitchen knife to make the peppers look decorative. Rub a little salt , lemon juice and ginger paste on the inner surface. Keep them upside down. Pour some oil on the outer surface. Rub the oil on the outer and inner surface and keep aside for 10 minutes.
2. For stuffing, heat butter in a heavy bottomed pan and fry the onions till transparent.
3. Add beans and carrots and stir fry for 2-3 minutes.
4. Drain the rice. Add rice and tomato puree. Stir fry gently for 2 minutes.
5. Add 2 cups water. Add salt and pepper. Boil. Cook covered on low flame for 10-12 minutes, till the rice is cooked. Remove from fire.
6. Sprinkle cheese all over on the rice. Do not stir. Cover and keep aside. The cheese melts and goes into the rice. Cool the rice mixture to stuff the peppers. Fill the peppers with this mixture.
7. Press well and keep aside till serving time. At the time of serving, heat a non stick pan or a flat bottomed kadhai. Put 2 tbsp oil and spread the oil to coat the pan.
8. Arrange filled peppers and cook covered on low heat for 5-7 minutes, changing the sides once or twice in-between, till the peppers get cooked and turn blackish at some places. Do not cook for a longer time as they will turn limp on doing so. Remove from pan. Sprinkle some cheese on top. Dot with tomato sauce and a sprig of parsley or mint. Serve.

Note: You may also microwave or cook peppers in a moderately hot oven at 180°C for 10 minutes. A few tomatoes can also be stuffed the same way to add colour to the pepper platter. Cook them only for 4 minutes or they tun limp.

Ajwaini Aloo Mirch

A quick dry vegetable, strongly flavoured with carom seeds.

Serves 4

2 large potatoes - cut into thin long fingers
3 capsicums - cut into thin long fingers
2 tbsp oil
1 tsp ajwain
5-6 flakes garlic crushed or 1 tsp finely chopped ginger
3 tomatoes (250 gm) - grind to a puree
¼ tsp haldi
2 tsp dhania powder
1 tsp salt
½ tsp red chilli powder
½ tsp garam masala
1 tbsp tomato ketchup

1. Cut potatoes into thin fingers like potato chips. Soak in cold water to which 1 tsp salt has been added. Soak for 10 minutes. Drain and wipe dry. Deep fry all together on medium flame till golden brown and cooked. Keep aside.
2. Heat 2 tbsp oil. Add ajwain. Wait for a minute.
3. Add garlic or ginger. Let it change colour.
4. Add fresh tomato puree. Stir for 5-6 minutes till dry.
5. Add all masalas - haldi, dhania, salt, red chilli and garam masala. Stir till oil separates.
6. Add tomato ketchup. Add 2 tbsp water. Mix.
7. Add capsicums. Stir for 2 minutes.
8. Add the fried potatoes. Stir to mix well. Serve hot as a side dish.

Note: Make the potato chips well browned and crisp.

Bharwaan Dal Mirch

The regular potato filling made crunchier by the addition of channe ki dal.

Serves 6-8

4 large simla mirch (capsicums)
2 tbsp lemon juice, 1 tsp ginger paste, 1 tbsp oil, ¾ tsp salt

FILLING
2 tbsp channa dal (split gram) - soaked in water for 15 minutes or more
3 potatoes - boiled & mashed roughly
1 tomato - pulp removed & finely chopped
2 tbsp dhania (fresh coriander) - finely chopped
2 tbsp oil
1 tsp jeera (cumin seeds)
2 onions - chopped finely
½ tsp haldi powder, 1 tsp dhania (coriander) powder, ¼ tsp amchoor (dried mango powder), ½ tsp garam masala, ½ tsp red chilli powder
½ tsp salt, or to taste

1. Cut a slice from the top of the capsicums. Scoop out the seeds and make it hollow. Rub some lemon juice, ginger paste, salt and oil on the inner surface. Keep them upside down for 10 minutes.
2. Boil channa dal in a little water for about 10 minutes, till very soft. Strain.
3. Heat 2 tbsp oil. Add jeera. When it crackles, add chopped onion. Stir fry till light brown.
4. Add boiled dal. Stir fry for a minute. Reduce flame. Add haldi, dhania powder, amchoor, garam masala and chilli powder. Mix for a minute.
5. Add roughly mashed potatoes and salt to taste. Stir fry for 4-5 minute till potatoes are well done. Add chopped coriander and pulp of tomato. Stir till it dries. Add pieces of tomato. Mix well.
6. Fill the capsicums with this mixture. Press well and keep aside till serving time.
7. Heat a non stick pan or a flat bottomed kadhai. Put 2 tbsp oil and spread the oil to coat the pan.
8. Arrange the filled capsicum and cook covered on low heat for 8-10 minutes, changing the sides once or twice in-between, till the capsicums get cooked and turn blackish at some places. Do not cook for a longer time as they will turn limp on doing so. Remove from pan. Cut into two halves and serve.

Kachumber Gobhi : Recipe on page 15 ➢
Saunfiyan Tori Tukri : Recipe on page 112 ➢

Mirch Lazeez

Capsicums with crisp golden potatoes with a wonderful spice blend.

Serves 4-5

3-4 capsicums - cut into 8-12 pieces (1" cubes)
2 potatoes - boiled & each cut into 8 pieces (1" cubes)
2 tomatoes - cut into 8 pieces (1" cubes)
juice of 1 lemon (2 tbsp)
3 tbsp oil
½ tsp jeera
1" piece ginger - chopped
¼ tsp haldi
1 tsp salt, or to taste

FLAVOURFUL MASALA
seeds of 3 chhoti illaichi (green cardamoms)
2-3 laung (cloves)
seeds of 2 moti illaichi (black cardamom)
1" stick dalchini (cinnamon)

1. Crush all ingredients of the flavourful masala to a rough powder.
2. Heat oil in a kadhai. Add jeera. Let it turn golden.
3. Add ginger. Add haldi.
4. Add potatoes and bhuno for 5-6 minutes till crisp and golden. Keep the potatoes spread out in the kadhai. Do not overlap them and do not stir too often. Let them turn crisp.
5. Add capsicum and tomatoes together. Add 1 tsp salt (or to taste) and 1 tsp flavourful masala. Stir fry for 2-3 minutes on low heat.
6. Squeeze lemon juice. Cook for 3-4 minutes till capsicums turn slightly soft. Serve.

Matar

(PEAS)

Khoya Matar Makhaana

Puffed lotus seeds with peas in a rich gravy.

Picture on page 127   *Serves 4*

1 cup shelled peas
100 gms khoya (dried whole milk)
1¼ cup makhaanas (puffed lotus seeds)
1 tbsp khus khus (poppy seeds) - soak for 15 minutes and grind to a paste
3 tomatoes - pureed in a mixer
1 tsp dhania powder (coriander powder)
½ tsp red chilli powder
½ tsp garam masala
salt to taste
1 tbsp kishmish (raisins)

GRIND TO A PASTE
2 big onions
1" piece ginger
2 green chillies
1 tbsp chopped coriander

1. Fry makhaanas to a golden brown colour in oil.
2. Grind onions, ginger, chillies and coriander leaves with a little water in a grinder.
3. Soak khus khus for 10-15 minutes and grind to a smooth paste.
4. Heat 4 tbsp oil. Add the onion-ginger paste. Cook on low heat till oil separates.
5. Add the khus khus paste. Cook for 1-2 minutes.
6. Add tomatoes pureed in a grinder. Cook till oil separates.
7. Add dhania powder, red chilli powder and garam masala.
8. Grate khoya. Add khoya and mix well for 1 minute.
9. Add peas and makhaanas. Mix well.
10. Add kishmish, peas and salt.
11. Add enough water to get a thick gravy. Cook covered till done.
12. Add makhanas. Give 1- 2 quick boils.
13. Serve hot, garnished with grated khoya.

Tip: Keep the khus khus in the fridge.

Lachhedaar Matar

A dry preparation of peas with onion rings.

Serves 4

2 cups shelled peas - boiled or frozen
3 tbsp oil, 1 tsp jeera
3 onions - cut into rings
½" piece ginger - finely chopped
¾ tsp garam masala, ½ tsp red chilli powder, 1 tsp dhania powder, ¼ tsp amchoor
1 tomato - grind to a puree, 2 tomatoes - chopped finely
1 green chilli - deseeded & slit lengthwise, optional
¾ tsp salt or to taste, 2 tbsp fresh coriander - chopped

1. Heat 3 tbsp oil in a kadhai, add jeera. Let it turn golden.
2. Add onion rings and stir till golden.
3. Add ginger and saute over medium heat for ½ minute.
4. Add pureed tomato, garam masala, red chilli powder, dhania powder and amchoor. Saute for 3-4 minutes till puree turns dry.
5. Add the boiled green peas and mix well. Add salt. Saute for 5 minutes.
6. Add chopped tomatoes and green chillies. Add green coriander. Stir fry for 3-4 minutes. Serve hot with paranthas or roti.

Matar Dhania Wale

Peas with a green coriander paste.

Serves 4-5

2 cups shelled peas
1 tbsp oil, a pinch of hing, ½ tsp jeera, ¼ tsp kalonji, ½ tsp salt, or to taste
1 firm tomato - cut into 8 pieces and pulp removed

DHANIA CHUTNEY
2 cups chopped coriander leaves, 4 flakes garlic, 1½" piece of ginger
2 green chillies, juice of 1 lemon, 1 tomato, ½ tsp salt, or to taste

1. Grind together all the ingredients of the dhania chutney.
2. Heat 1 tbsp oil in the pressure cooker. Add hing, jeera and kalonji.
3. When jeera turns brown, add peas. Bhuno for 2-3 minutes.
4. Add dhania chutney to the peas & mix well. Add salt. Pressure cook to give 1 whistle. Open the cooker after the pressure drops. Mix in the tomato. Serve hot.

Matar Tamatar in Cashew Gravy

Peas with tomatoes in a rich white gravy, flavoured with green cardamoms and fenugreek.

Picture on page 31   *Serves 4*

1½ cups boiled or frozen peas
1 small firm tomato - cut into 4 pieces
4 tbsp cashewnuts - soaked in ½ cup hot water for 5 minutes
4 tbsp dahi
3 tbsp oil
½ tsp jeera (cumin seeds)
1 tbsp kasoori methi
2 onions and 1" piece ginger - ground to a paste
1 tsp garam masala
½ tsp red chilli powder
1 tsp salt, or to taste
½ cup cream mixed with ½ cup milk
seeds of 3 chhoti illaichi (green cardamoms) - crushed
1 tsp tandoori masala

1. Drain cashewnuts and grind along with curd to a fine paste.
2. Heat 3 tbsp oil. Add jeera. Wait till it turns golden.
3. Add onion and ginger paste. Stir fry onion paste on low flame till oil separates and it turns light golden.
4. Gradually add curd-cashewnut mixture, stirring continuously. Bhuno for 4-5 minutes till masala turns thick and oil separates.
5. Add kasoori methi, garam masala, red chilli and salt. Stir for 1-2 minutes.
6. Reduce heat. Add cream mixed with milk. Stir to mix well.
7. Add 2 cups water. Boil. Simmer for 5-7 minutes, on low flame till gravy turns a little thick.
8. Reduce heat. Add boiled peas and chhoti illaichi. Stir for 2-3 minutes.
9. Add tomato pieces & tandoori masala. Mix well. Remove from fire & serve hot.

Note: The milk should be added after reducing the flame. While the milk is being added, always keep stirring and keep the heat very low. Never boil the gravy too much after the milk has been added. It might curdle if done so.

Chhote Bhutte

(BABYCORN)

Makhani Mirch Makai

Green chillies and baby corns in a simple yet delicious gravy.

Picture on page 79   *Serves 5-6*

10-12 pieces (150 gm) baby corns - cut lengthwise into 2 long pieces
6 big green chillies - slit & deseeded
1 large onion - ground to a paste
2 tbsp cashews - soaked in warm water and ground to a paste
4 tomatoes - ground to a puree
1" piece ginger - grated
4 tbsp oil
¼ tsp haldi, 1 tsp dhania powder (ground coriander), ½ tsp garam masala
1¼ tsp salt, or to taste, ½ tsp red chilli powder
1 cup water
1 cup milk, see note
½ cup cream (optional)

1. Heat 4 tbsp oil. Add green chillies and fry for 3-4 minutes till they turn slightly whitish. Remove from oil and keep aside.
2. Add baby corns and fry for 3-4 minutes till brown specs appear. Remove from oil and keep aside.
3. Heat the remaining oil. Add onion, fry till light brown.
4. Add haldi, dhania powder and garam masala. Stir for a minute.
5. Add fresh tomato puree. Cook for 5 minutes on low heat till dry and oil separates.
6. Add cashew paste. Mix.
7. Add water and boil. Add salt and pepper to taste. Add fried baby corns. Simmer on low flame for 10 minutes till thick.
8. Add grated ginger. Remove from fire and keep aside till serving time.
9. At serving time, add milk to the thick masala to get a gravy. Mix well. Keep on low heat, stirring continuously till it comes to a boil.
10. Add fried green chillies and cream. Remove from heat immediately and serve.

Note: The milk should never be added to the hot tomato gravy. Let it cool down before adding the milk. Never boil the gravy too much after the milk has been added. It might curdle if done so.

Choose green chillies which are thick, big and light green, as the small, dark green ones are hotter. Remember, to deseed them. After deseeding them, tap them gently to remove all the seeds.

Baby Corn Bullets

Whole baby corns coated with a yogurt marinade and cooked till golden.

Serves 4-5   *Picture on page 59*

200 gm thick baby corns - keep whole
juice of ½ lemon
1-2 capsicums - cut into large 1" pieces
8 cherry tomatoes or 1 large tomato - cut into 8 pieces & pulp removed
1 onion - cut into fours & separated or 4 spring onions (keep white part whole)
1-2 tbsp melted butter for basting
some chaat masala - to sprinkle

MARINADE
1½ cups thick curd - hang for 30 minutes
1 tbsp cornflour
2 tbsp thick cream or malai
¼ tsp ajwain (carom seeds)
1 tbsp thick ginger-garlic paste (squeeze out the liquid)
½ tsp kala namak (black salt), ¼ tsp haldi
1 tbsp tandoori or barbecue masala, ¼ tsp red chilli powder, ¾ tsp salt

1. Boil 4-5 cups water with 2 tsp salt, ¼ tsp haldi and juice of ½ lemon. Add baby corns to boiling water. After the boil returns, boil for 1 minute or till slightly soft. Strain and wipe dry the corns on a clean kitchen towel. Keep aside.
2. Mix all ingredients of the marinade in a large bowl.
3. Rub oil generously on a wire rack or grill of the oven.
4. Add baby corns first to the marinade in the bowl and mix well to coat the marinade. Remove from bowl and arrange on the greased rack. In the remaining marinade in the bowl, add onion, capsicum and tomatoes. Leave these in the bowl itself. Marinate all for atleast ½ hour.
5. Grill baby corns first in an oven at 200°C for 15 minutes or roast in a gas tandoor. Pour a little melted butter on them to baste them, so that they keep moist. Put the onion and capsicum also along with the corns and grill for 10 minutes. Lastly put the tomatoes in the oven with the onion-capsicum and grill further for 2-3 minutes.
6. Serve sprinkled with some chat masala, along with lemon wedges.

Note: If you do not want to do cook them in the oven, simply heat 2 tbsp oil in a kadhai. Add all the marinated vegetables in the hot oil and stir on high flame till coated well with the marinade and golden brown.

Kadhai Baby Corns

Corns in the usual kadhai masala, flavoured with fenugreek and coriander. The addition of some milk at the end makes all the difference.

Serves 4

200 gm baby corns (20 pieces approx.)
juice of ½ lemon
2 capsicums - cut into fingers
1-2 dry red chillies
1½ tsp saboot dhania (coriander seeds)
a pinch of methi daana (fenugreek seeds)
2 tsp ginger- garlic paste
2 onions - chopped
4 tomatoes - pureed in a grinder
1 tbsp kasoori methi (dry fenugreek leaves)
¼ tsp haldi, ½ tsp garam masala
½ tsp amchoor, 1¼ tsp salt, or to taste
½" piece ginger - cut into match sticks or shredded on the grater (1 tsp)
5 tbsp oil

1. Boil 4 cups water with 2 tsp salt and lemon juice. Add baby corns and boil for 2 minutes. Drain. Refresh in cold water. Cut into 2 pieces lengthwise.
2. Warm red chillies and dhania saboot on a tawa, till slightly crisp and dry, for about 30 seconds.
3. Roughly grind red chillies and saboot dhania to a rough powder.
4. Heat 2 tbsp oil in a kadhai and add the boiled baby corns. Bhuno for 4-5 minutes till they start turning brown. Keep them spaced out while bhunoing and let them not overlap each other. Add the capsicum strips and stir fry for 2 minutes. Remove from kadhai and keep aside.
5. Heat 3 tbsp oil in a kadhai. Reduce flame. Add a pinch of methi daana, dhania-red chilli powder. Stir for 30 seconds. Add garlic or ginger paste.
6. Add onion. Cook till onions turn light golden.
7. Add tomatoes and stir for about 4-5 minutes on low heat till dry.
8. Add salt, kasoori methi, haldi, garam masala and amchoor. Mix well till oil separates. Add ½ cup water. Let it boil.
9. Add baby corns and capsicum. Cook for 2-3 minutes.
10. Reduce heat. Mix in the shredded ginger. Remove from fire. Serve hot.

Matar Tamatar in Cashew Gravy : Recipe on page 26 ➤
Special Palak Paneer : Recipe on page 36 ➤
Kadhai Bhindi Aur Aloo : Recipe on page 39 ➤

Badaami Baby Corns

Baby corns in a red almond gravy. If baby corns are not available, regular corn on the cob can be used instead.

Serves 8

200 gm baby corns or 2 small tender bhutte (corn on the cobs)
½-1 cup milk, approx.
2-3 tbsp almonds (badam) - boiled in hot water, peeled (blanched) and ground to a paste with ¼ cup water

MASALA

2 small onions, 4 tomatoes, 1" piece ginger, 1 green chilli - grind to a paste
4 tbsp oil, ½ tsp royal black cumin (shah jeera)
1 tsp dhania (coriander) powder, ½ tsp amchoor, 1½ tsp salt
½ tsp red chilli powder, 1 tsp garam masala, 1 tsp tandoori masala
2-3 chhoti illaichi (green cardamom) - seeds crushed
50 -100 gms paneer - grated (½-1 cup), 3 tbsp chopped coriander

BAGHAR OR TEMPERING

1 tbsp desi ghee or oil, ½ tsp shah jeera (black cumin), 1 tsp finely chopped ginger
5-6 almonds (badaam) - cut into thin long pieces, ¼ tsp red chilli powder

1. Choose small baby corns or thin tender bhuttas. Keep baby corns whole or cut each bhutta into 4 small pieces. If thick, slit each piece into two.
2. Put all the pieces of baby corns, 1 tsp sugar, ¼ tsp haldi and ½ cup milk in a pan. Give one boil and keep on low heat for 2 minutes. If using bhuttas, use a pressure cooker to cook them. Pressure cook bhutta pieces with 1 cup milk to give one whistle. Then keep on low flame for 5 minutes. Remove from fire.
3. Grind onions, tomatoes, green chilli and ginger to a paste in a grinder.
4. Heat 4 tbsp oil. Add shah jeera. After a minute, add onion-tomato paste and cook till dry and oil separates. Reduce flame. Add red chilli powder, dhania, amchoor, salt and garam masala. Cook for 1 minute.
5. Add almond paste. Stir to mix well.
6. Keeping the flame low, add the left over milk from the boiled bhuttas, stirring continuously. Stir for 2-3 minutes.
7. Add corn and simmer on low flame for 3 minutes. Add enough (2-3 cups approx.) water to get a thin gravy. Boil. Simmer for 5-7 minutes till slightly thick. Add tandoori masala, chhoti illaichi, grated paneer and coriander.
8. Transfer to a serving dish. For the baghar, heat ghee or oil. Add shah jeera and ginger. After a few seconds, add almonds and stir. Add red chilli powder, remove from fire and pour the oil on the gravy. Serve.

Paalak

(SPINACH)

Haryaali Malai Kofta

Stuffed paneer koftas in spinach gravy.

Serves 6-8

KOFTAS (12-13)
100 gm paneer - grated and mashed, 2 big pinches baking powder
2 slices bread - remove sides, 2 tbsp curd
1 green chilli - chopped finely, 1 tbsp finely chopped coriander
½ tsp salt & ½ tsp pepper, ¼ tsp red chill powder, to taste
1½ tbsp maida (plain flour), 3-4 cashewnuts & 3-4 kishmish - chopped

BOIL TOGETHER
½ kg spinach - chop only leaves, 1 green chilli - chopped
1" piece ginger - chopped

GRIND TOGETHER FOR GRAVY
2 onions, 2 tomatoes, 2 laung (cloves)

OTHER INGREDIENTS FOR GRAVY
4 tbsp oil, ¾ tsp salt, or to taste
1 tsp dhania powder, ½ tsp red chilli powder, ¼ tsp garam masala

TADKA/TEMPERING
1 tbsp desi ghee, 1" piece ginger - cut into match sticks
1 green chilli - slit lengthways, ½ tsp red chilli powder

1. To prepare koftas, spread 1 tbsp curd on each slice of bread to wet it. After spreading curd on both sides of bread, keep aside for a minute.
2. Mash the paneer well. Add baking powder, green chillies and coriander.
3. Mash the bread slices well and mix with the paneer. Add salt, pepper and red chilli powder to taste.
4. Add maida in the end. Mix well but lightly.
5. Make balls and stuff a few pieces of cashews & kishmish in the centre.
6. Deep fry 4-5 pieces at a time, in medium hot oil and keep aside.
7. To prepare the gravy, wash palak leaves and chop roughly. Put leaves with a green chilli and ginger in a pan and cook covered for 3-4 minutes after it boils. Remove from fire. Cool.
8. After the spinach cools, blend to a paste and keep aside.
9. Heat 4 tbsp oil. Add the onion - tomato paste and cook stirring till dry.
10. Add masalas - dhania powder, red chilli powder, amchoor and about ¾ tsp salt, or to taste. Bhuno further for 1-2 minutes on low flame, till oil separates.

11. Add the ground spinach and bhuno for 5-7 minutes. Add ½-1 cup water to make a thin green gravy and boil for 4-5 minutes on low heat.
12. At serving time heat the spinach gravy and add koftas. Stir gently on low flame for 1-2 minutes till the koftas are heated through. Remove from fire and transfer to a serving dish.
13. For the tadka, heat 1 tbsp desi ghee and add the ginger. When it turns brownish, shut off the flame. Add green chillies. Add red chilli powder and immediately pour the oil on the koftas in the serving dish. Mix lightly. Serve.

Achaari Palak Makai

Spinach combined with corn kernels and tempered with pickle spices.

Serves 4

½ cup boiled or tinned corn kernels (makai ke dane)
1 bundle spinach (700 gm) - chopped finely without the stems
1 tbsp kasoori methi, ½ tsp sugar, ½ cup water
½ cup chopped coriander, 2 green chillies, 1" piece ginger - chopped
3 tbsp oil
2 onions - ground to a paste, 3 tomatoes - ground to a puree
¼ tsp haldi, 1 tsp salt, 2 tsp dhania powder, ½ tsp garam masala
1 cup milk

ACHAARI TADKA
2 tbsp oil
½ tsp saunf, ½ tsp jeera, ½ tsp rai or sarson, ¼ tsp kalonji, a pinch of methi daana
2 dry red chillies, ¼ tsp red chilli powder, preferably degi mirch

1. Mix chopped spinach with kasoori methi and sugar in a deep pan. Add ½ cup water and bring to a boil. Cook uncovered till soft, for about 4-5 minutes on low heat, stirring in-between. Remove from fire. Cool. Grind the spinach along with the liquid, ½ cup coriander, green chillies and ginger to a puree. Keep aside.
2. Heat 3 tbsp oil. Add onion paste and stir till golden brown. Add tomatoes and cook till dry. Add haldi, salt, dhania powder & garam masala. Stir till oil separates.
3. Add corn and stir for 2 minutes. Add spinach paste and cook for 10 minutes.
4. Add milk and stir on low heat for 2 minutes. Remove to a serving dish.
5. For the tadka, heat oil or ghee. Reduce heat. Collect together saunf, jeera, rai or sarson, kalonji and methi daana. Add all these together to the oil. When methi daana turns brown, add the dry red chillies and chilli powder. Remove from fire and pour over the spinach in the dish.

Special Palak Paneer

The addition of green coriander and kasoori methi to spinach makes it taste special. The paneer is flavoured with fennel coated batter and then dropped in the spinach puree. If you wish, you can avoid frying the paneer.

Picture on page 31   *Serves 4*

200 gms paneer - cut into 8 big pieces
500 gms paalak (spinach) - chopped without stalks (5 cups)
4 tbsp kasoori methi (dry fenugreek leaves)
1 cup chopped coriander, 1 green chilli, 1 tsp sugar
2 tbsp besan (gram flour)
½ stick dalchini (cinnamon), 2 chhoti illaichi (green cardamoms), 3-4 laung (cloves)
5 tbsp oil
2 onions - ground to a paste
½ cup cream or milk, approx., 1 tsp salt, or to taste

BAGHAR
1 tbsp desi ghee, 1 tbsp chopped ginger, ½ tsp red chilli powder

BATTER FOR FRYING PANEER
6 tbsp besan, ½ tsp salt and ½ tsp pepper
1 tsp saunf (fennel)- crushed, ½ cup water

1.   Boil spinach, kasoori methi, fresh coriander and green chilli in 1 cup water with sugar. Cook on low flame for 4-5 minutes till spinach turns soft. Remove from fire.
2.   Strain the spinach and keep the liquid aside. Mix besan with the spinach liquid and keep aside.
3.   Cool the spinach and blend to a puree.
4.   In another bowl mix all the ingredients of the batter.
5.   Dip paneer pieces in batter & deep fry till golden brown. Keep aside.
6.   Crush dalchini, laung and seeds of chhoti illaichi to a rough powder. Keep aside.
7.   Heat 5 tbsp oil. Add onions and cook on low heat till they turn light brown.
8.   Add the freshly ground masala. Cook for a few seconds.
9.   Add besan dissolved in liquid. Cook for 2 minutes.
10. Add the palak puree. Bhuno for 5-7 minutes till dry and oil separates.
11. Add enough cream or milk, to get the right consistency and colour. Cook on low heat for 2 minutes.
12. Add the batter fried paneer pieces and salt to taste. Simmer for few minutes.
13. To serve, heat 1 tbsp desi ghee for the baghar. Add ginger. Remove from fire. When ginger turns golden, add red chilli powder to the hot oil. Remove from fire and mix lightly with the spinach. Serve hot.

Paalak Mushrooms

Serves 3-4

100 gm mushrooms - small in size
juice of ½ lemon, 1 tsp salt
1 tbsp butter

PRESSURE COOK TOGETHER
½ kg paalak (spinach), ¾ cup water
1" piece ginger - chopped, 3-4 flakes garlic - chopped, 1 green chilli - chopped

TOMATO PASTE
2 tomatoes, ½" piece ginger, 1 green chilli, 3-4 flakes garlic

OTHER INGREDIENTS
3 tbsp oil
3 onions - ground to a paste
¼ tsp black pepper, ½ tsp salt, or to taste, ½ tsp garam masala
seeds of 1 moti illaichi (brown cardamom) - crushed roughly
seeds of 1 chhoti illaichi (green cardamom) - crushed roughly

BAGHAR (OPTIONAL)
1 tsp desi ghee, ¼ tsp red chilli powder

1. Chop paalak leaves, discarding the stalks. Wash in plenty of water. Pressure cook paalak with all the ingredients to give one whistle. Keep on low flame for 5-7 minutes. Cool and blend in a mixer.
2. Slice tip of the mushroom stalk and wash to remove dirt. Boil 2 cups water with 1 tsp salt and lemon juice. Remove from fire. Soak mushrooms in it for 5 minutes.
3. Drain mushrooms and wipe dry on a kitchen towel.
4. Heat 1 tbsp butter. Add the mushrooms and stir fry for 4-5 minutes till the mushrooms turn light golden. Keep aside.
5. Grind tomatoes, ginger, green chilli and garlic to a paste. Grind onions separately to a paste.
6. Heat 3 tbsp oil in a kadhai. Add onion paste and cook stirring till golden brown.
7. Add fresh tomato paste. Cook till dry and oil separates.
8. Add black pepper, moti illaichi, chhoti illaichi, salt and ½ tsp garam masala. Bhuno for ½ minute.
9. Add spinach and cook for 4-5 minutes on low flame till oil separates.
10. Add mushrooms. Cook for 2 minutes. Transfer to a serving dish.
11. For the baghar, heat 1 tsp of desi ghee. Remove from fire. Add ¼ tsp red chilli powder and pour the hot oil on the hot paalak. Serve hot.

Bhindi
(LADY'S FINGER)

Kadhai Bhindi aur Aloo

An interesting combination of lady's fingers with potato fingers.

Serves 4   *Picture on page 31*

300 gm small sized bhindi (lady's finger)
2 potatoes - cut into thin fingers
3-4 flakes garlic - crushed roughly
2 tbsp ready made tomato puree
1 tsp kasoori methi (dry fenugreek leaves)
1½ tsp dhania powder, ½ tsp garam masala, ¾ tsp salt
½ tsp red chilli powder
¼ tsp sugar
oil to fry

1. Wash bhindi. Wipe with a clean kitchen towel. Cut the tip of the head of each bhindi. Leave the pointed end as it is.
2. Heat some oil for deep frying in a kadhai to medium hot temperature. Add half of the bhindi and fry on medium flame for about 5 minutes till it gets cooked. Remove from oil.
3. Fry the second batch of bhindi also.
4. Deep fry the potato fingers to a golden brown colour on medium flame till it gets cooked and golden.
5. Remove all the oil from the kadhai. Heat 2 tbsp oil again in the kadhai.
6. Reduce flame. Add garlic and fry till it changes colour. Remove from fire.
7. Add tomato puree, kasoori methi, 1½ tsp dhania powder, ½ tsp garam masala, ¾ tsp salt, ½ tsp red chilli powder and ¼ tsp sugar.
8. Return to fire. Stir for 1-2 minutes on low flame.
9. Add the fried potatoes. Mix. Add the bhindi. Stir for a few minutes. Cover and cook on low flame for 3-4 minutes. Serve.

Hyderabadi Bhindi

Masala coated lady's fingers with the flavour of South India.

Serves 4

250 gm bhindi

MASALA
2 tbsp oil
1 tsp channa dal
1 tsp urad dal
½ tsp jeera (cumin seeds)
½ tsp sarson (mustard seeds)
2 dry, red chillies - broken into pieces
10-12 curry pattas
1 green chilli - deseeded & chopped
1 large onion - chopped
2 tomatoes - chopped
½ tsp dhania (coriander) powder
¼ tsp chilli powder
¾ tsp salt, or to taste
a pinch of haldi
3 tbsp thick curd - beat till smooth
grated fresh coconut for garnish, optional

1. Wash bhindi and wipe dry. Cut the tip of the head of each bhindi, leaving the pointed end as it is. Now cut the bhindi vertically from the middle making 2 smaller pieces from each bhindi. Heat oil in a kadhai and deep fry the bhindi on medium heat in 2 batches. Do not over fry the bhindi, it should retain it's green colour. Drain on a paper napkin. Keep aside.
2. Heat 2 tbsp oil in a pan. Reduce heat. Add both the dals and stir for a few seconds till dals change colour.
3. Add jeera, sarson and dry, red chillies.
4. Stir & add curry patta, green chilli and onions. Cook till onion turns light golden.
5. Add the tomatoes and cook for 2 minutes till soft.
6. Add the dry masalas - dhania powder, red chilli powder, salt and haldi. Bhuno the masalas for 2 minutes.
7. Add ¼ cup water and the fried bhindi. Cover and cook for 1 minute.
8. Add curd. Cook on medium heat till the water from the curd evaporates.
9. Stir for 3-4 minutes till the masala coats the bhindi.
10. Garnish with grated coconut if you like. Serve with chappati and a raita.

Besani Bhindi

Lady's fingers coated with gramflour and flavoured subtly with fennel.

Serves 4

250 gm bhindi (lady finger) - small & tender
2-3 small onions - cut into four & separated
3 tbsp oil

POWDERED MASALA
¾ tsp salt
½ tsp red chilli powder
1 tsp dhania (coriander) powder
½ tsp garam masala
½ tsp haldi
1 tsp amchoor (dried mango powder)

OTHER INGREDIENTS
1½ tsp ginger paste
2 tbsp besan (gram flour)
½ tsp saunf (fennel)

1. Wash, drain bhindi. Wipe dry with a clean kitchen towel.
2. Slice off ¼" from the top and the base of each bhindi. Make a slit in each piece. Keep the bhindi in a shallow bowl or a large pan.
3. Mix all ingredients of the powdered masala together.
4. Sprinkle this masala over the bhindi.
5. Heat 3 tbsp oil in a big kadhai. Add saunf. Reduce flame.
6. When it changes colour, add besan. Cook on low flame till it changes colour.
7. Add ginger paste. Stir for a few seconds. Add the bhindi and the onions
8. Cook for 15 minutes on medium flame, stirring occasionally till completely cooked.

Kurkuri Ajwaini Bhindi

Amazingly crisp and crunchy with a strong flavour of carom seeds.

Serves 2-3

250 gm bhindi (lady fingers)
1 tsp ajwain (carom seeds)
¼ tsp haldi
2 tsp chaat masala
1 tsp chilli powder
1 tsp ginger or garlic paste
3 tbsp besan (gram flour)
½ tsp salt, or to taste
juice of ½ lemon (1 tbsp)
oil for frying

1. Wash and pat dry bhindi. Cut the head. Cut the bhindi into four lengthwise to get 4 long pieces from each bhindi. Place in a shallow bowl or paraat.
2. Heat oil in a kadhai for frying.
3. Sprinkle ajwain, haldi, chaat masala, ginger or garlic paste, dry besan and salt on the bhindi.
4. Sprinkle lemon juice and mix well to coat the bhindi with the spices.
5. Add half of the bhindi to hot oil and fry in 2 batches till crisp. Drain on absorbent paper.

Tip: Mix all the ingredients to the bhindi at the time of frying as the salt added releases moisture which can make the bhindi soggy.

Gajar

(CARROT)

Kastoori Gajar Matar

Dry fenugreek is mixed with carrots and some green peas to make a very colourful dish. Milk is added to dry fenugreek leaves to freshen them.

Serves 4

3 carrots - cut into ¼" cubes (1½ cups chopped)
1 packet (2 cups) kasoori methi (dried fenugreek leaves) - cleaned & soaked in water for ½ hour
1½ cups shelled peas - boiled
1 cup milk
2 tbsp mustard oil or any refined oil
a pinch of sugar
1 tsp salt
½ tsp red chilli
½ tsp garam masala
a pinch of amchoor (dried mango powder)

1. Soak cleaned methi in water for at least ½ hour or even more. Strain and keep aside.
2. Heat oil in a heavy bottomed kadhai.
3. Add kasoori methi and milk. Cook till completely dry. Add a pinch of sugar. Mix well.
4. Add salt and red chilli powder. Cook for 1 minute.
5. Add carrots. Stir fry for 1-2 minutes on low flame.
6. Cover and cook, sprinkling water in-between, on low flame till carrots are done.
7. Add peas. Add garam masala and amchoor. Uncover and stir fry for 2-3 minutes.
8. At serving time, add ¼ cup milk if it seems too dry and heat the vegetable well. Serve hot.

Gajar Paneer Jalfrezi

Paneer deliciously combined with carrots to make a semi dry vegetable.

Serves 4-5   *Picture on Page 1*

200 gm paneer - cut into thin long pieces
250 gms (3-4) carrots - cut diagonally into very thin slices
1 long, firm tomato - cut into 4, pulp removed and cut into thin long pieces
15-20 curry leaves
4 tbsp oil

COLLECT TOGETHER
½ tsp jeera (cumin seeds)
½ tsp sarson (mustard seeds)
¾ tsp kalonji (½ tsp plus ¼ tsp)(onion seeds)
¼ tsp methi daana (fenugreek seeds)

MIX TOGETHER
5 tbsp tomato puree
2 tbsp tomato ketchup
2 tsp ginger-garlic paste or 2 tsp ginger-garlic - finely chopped
½ tsp red chilli powder
½ tsp amchoor powder
1¼ tsp dhania powder
1 tsp salt, or to taste

1. Mix together - tomato puree, tomato ketchup, ginger, garlic, red chilli powder, dhania powder, amchoor and salt in a bowl. Keep aside.
2. Heat 3 tbsp oil in a kadhai. Add the collected seeds together. When jeera turns golden, reduce heat and add curry leaves and stir for a few seconds.
3. Add the tomato puree mixed with dry masalas and stir on low heat for 2 minutes.
4. Add carrots. Stir for 2-3 minutes.
5. Add ¼ cup water. Cover the kadhai. Cook on low heat for about 4-5 minutes, till carrot is tender, but still remains crunchy at the same time.
6. Add paneer and tomato slices. Stir till well blended. Remove from fire.

Note: 1 capsicum can also be added to add colour to the dish. Add capsicum cut into thin fingers after the carrot is done. Saute capsicum for a minute and then add the paneer.

Gajar Methi

Try carrots with methi instead of the usual potatoes. The addition of garlic is optional.

Serves 4

2-3 carrots - peeled and cut into cubes
2 bunches (700 gm) fresh methi (fenugreek leaves)
4 tbsp mustard oil or any refined oil
3-4 flakes garlic - crushed
¼ tsp hing (asafoetida)
¾ tsp jeera (cumin)
1 tsp garam masala
½ tsp amchoor
1 tsp dhania powder
½ tsp red chilli powder
1½ tsp salt or to taste

1. Remove the hard stems of methi & chop very finely. Rub 1 tsp of salt & keep aside.
2. Peel and cut carrots into tiny cubes.
3. Wash methi in several changes of water till clean. Squeeze methi well to drain out water and keep aside.
4. Heat mustard oil to smoking point. Remove from fire. After a few seconds, add garlic and hing.
5. Return to fire. Reduce flame. Add jeera. Let it turn golden.
6. Add methi leaves. Stir fry till the water evaporates. Cook further for 5 minutes.
7. Add carrots and stir fry for a minute.
8. Add salt, dhania powder, red chilli powder, garam masala and amchoor. Cook covered for about 8-10 minutes till carrots turn soft. Serve hot.

Kofte Gajar Ke

Delicious carrot balls in a light gravy.

Serves 6-8   *Picture on page 49*

KOFTAS (16 BALLS)
250 gm (4) carrots - peeled & grated finely
2 boiled potatoes - grated, 2 green chillies - deseeded & chopped finely
2 tbsp cornflour, a pinch of baking powder
1 tsp salt, or to taste, ½ tsp red chilli powder, ½ tsp amchoor, ½ tsp garam masala
16 dry aloo bukhaaras (plums) - soaked for 20 minutes & deseeded or 16 kishmish

PASTE
3 onions, 3 red tomatoes, 2 green chillies, 8-10 flakes garlic, 1" piece ginger

GRAVY
3 tbsp oil
2 laung (cloves), 1 stick dalchini (cinnamon) - broken into 2-3 pieces
1 tbsp kasoori methi (dry fenugreek leaves)
½ tsp haldi, ½ tsp red chilli powder, ½ tsp garam masala
2 tsp dhania (coriander) powder, 1½ tsp salt or to taste, 2 tbsp coriander leaves
1 cup milk, see note

1. Grate carrots finely. Squeeze them. Mix all ingredients given under the koftas in a shallow bowl. Knead the mixture well for 4-5 minutes till well blended. Form into 1" long oval balls or round balls. Insert a deseeded, soaked dry aloo-bhukhaara or a kishmish. Shape into a ball again.

2. Heat oil to deep fry the balls. Add only 2-3 balls at a time and carefully fry them on **medium flame** till they turn golden and get cooked from inside.

3. To prepare the gravy, grind together onions, tomatoes, green chillies, garlic and ginger to a paste.

4. Heat 3 tbsp oil in a kadhai and fry dalchini and laung for a few seconds.

5. Add the onion and tomato paste. Cook till dry.

6. Add kasoori methi and all the dry masalas. Stir fry for 4-5 minutes till thick.

7. Add 2½ cups water to get a thin gravy. Boil. Add salt and coriander leaves. Simmer on low flame for 5-6 minutes. Keep aside till serving time.

8. At serving time, mix 1 cup milk to the gravy and now keep on low heat. Add koftas. Bring to a boil, stirring, on low heat. Serve hot with rice or chappatis.

Note: The milk should never be added to the hot tomato gravy. Let it cool down before adding the milk. Never boil the gravy too much after the milk has been added. It might curdle if done so.

Arbi

(COLOCASIA)

Kofte Gajar Ke : Recipe on page 47 ➤
Makki Matar Khumb : Recipe on page 57 ➤

Makhani Arbi

A very different style of preparing arbi in a delicious sauce. Ajwain elevates this delicacy from the ordinary to a gourmet's delight.

Serves 4

250 gm arbi (medium size)
2 tbsp besan (gram flour)
3 tbsp oil
½ tsp ajwain
1 onion - chopped
1 green chilli - slit, deseeded & chopped
½ tbsp grated ginger, 1 tbsp chopped coriander
½ tsp red chilli powder, ½ tsp salt or to taste
½ tbsp lemon juice, ¼ tsp garam masala

MAKHANI GRAVY
250 gm (4) tomatoes - chopped roughly
½ tsp ginger paste, ½ tsp garlic paste, 1 green chilli, ½ tsp red chilli powder
2 laung (cloves), 1 chhoti illaichi (green cardamom), salt to taste
1 tbsp butter, 1 tbsp fresh malai or cream, ½ tsp honey, 1 tsp kasoori methi

1. Pressure cook whole arbi with 3 cups water and 1 tsp salt to give one whistle. Keep on low flame for 2-3 minutes. Remove from fire. Cool and drain.
2. To prepare makhani gravy, put tomatoes in a pan, add 1 cup water, ginger and garlic paste, green chilli, red chilli powder, laung, chhoti illaichi. Boil. Cover and cook on low heat till it is reduced to a saucy consistency.
3. Remove from fire. Cool and blend to a puree. Strain the tomato puree through a sieve into a clean pan.
4. Add butter and cream. Stir.
5. Add salt and honey. Keep on fire. Boil. Simmer on low flame for 1-2 minutes.
6. Add kasoori methi and remove from fire. Keep makhani gravy aside.
7. Peel and flatten each piece of arbi. Sprinkle some salt and red chilli powder on it. Sprinkle dry besan. Over turn the pieces and sprinkle salt, red chilli and besan on this side too. Mix, so as to coat lightly.
8. Heat oil in a kadhai for deep frying. Deep fry arbi till well fried and crisp.
9. Heat 2 tbsp oil in a kadhai, add ajwain, when it turns golden, add chopped onions, grated ginger and green chillies and saute for 3 minutes. Add ½ tsp salt.
10. Add arbi, red chillies and ½ of the coriander. Bhuno for a minute.
11. Add the prepared makhani gravy and bhuno until the arbi is coated with the gravy. Adjust salt. Sprinkle lemon juice, garam masala and the remaining coriander. Stir well and serve immediately.

Arbi Ajwaini

Arbi combined with a masala of onion rings flavoured with carom seeds.

Serves 4

½ kg arbi (colocasia)
2 onions - cut into rings
½" piece ginger - chopped finely
2-3 green chillies - cut into thin long pieces
¼ tsp haldi
2 tomatoes - chopped
1 tsp ajwain (carom seeds)
½ tsp jeera (cumin seeds)
1 tsp dhania (coriander) powder
½ tsp salt, or to taste
½ tsp red chilli powder
½ tsp amchoor (dried mango powder)
½ cup chopped coriander

1. Pressure cook arbi with 3 cups water and 2 tsp salt to give one whistle. Keep on low flame for 4 minutes. Do not over boil. Peel and flatten each piece between the palms.
2. Heat 2 cups oil in a kadhai for frying. Put 4-5 pieces of flattened arbi at one time in oil. Fry till golden brown. Remove from oil. Keep aside.
3. Heat 2 tbsp oil in a clean kadhai. Reduce flame. Add ajwain and jeera. Cook till jeera turns golden.
4. Add onion rings and cook till soft. Add haldi and mix.
5. Add tomatoes and cook for 2 minutes till soft. Add ginger and stir for a minute.
6. Add chilli powder, amchoor, salt and dhania powder. Stir to mix well. Add 2-3 tbsp water. Boil.
7. Add fried arbi. Mix well.
8. Add hara dhania and green chillies. Stir fry for 2 minutes.

Note: If the arbi is not boiled in salted water, add a little extra salt.

Karaari Bharwaan Arbi

Picture on cover

Serves 8

½ kg arbi (colocasia) of medium size

STUFFING

½ tsp ajwain (carom seeds)
½ tsp kalaunji (onion seeds)
3/4 tsp red chilli powder, 3/4 tsp garam masala
2 tsp dhania (coriander) powder, 1 tsp amchoor, 1 tsp salt, 1 tsp oil

COATING

3 tbsp suji (semolina)
3 tbsp besan (gram flour)
¼ tsp each of salt, garam masala and red chilli powder

MASALA

2 onions - cut into fine rings, 2 capsicums - cut into fine rings
2 tbsp oil, ½ tsp ajwain (carom seeds), a pinch of haldi
½ tsp salt, ¼ tsp red chilli powder, 1 tsp lemon juice
1 tomato- cut into thin long pieces without pulp
½ tsp tandoori masala or chaat masala

1. Boil 4 cups water with 2 tsp salt. Add arbi to boiling water. After the boil comes again, cover and cook for about 12 minutes till arbi is done.
2. Drain. Cool the arbi and peel it.
3. Make a lengthways slit in each arbi.
4. Mix all ingredients of the stuffing, including the oil. The oil binds the stuffing.
5. Fill about ¼ tsp of stuffing in each slit with a spoon. Press the arbi to flatten it slightly and also to close the slit.
6. Repeat with all the pieces.
7. Heat oil in a kadhai for frying. Mix the coating ingredients in a flat plate.
8. Sprinkle some water on the stuffed arbi pieces. Roll each piece of arbi in the dry suji-besan mix and deep fry 5-6 pieces at one time on medium heat till golden.
9. For the masala- heat 2 tbsp oil in a pan, add ajwain, wait for a minute.
10. Add onions and fry till light golden, add a pinch of haldi.
11. Add salt, chilli powder & lemon juice. Mix. Add capsicum rings & cook for a minute.
12. Add fried arbi, stir fry for 2 minutes. Add tomatoes, mix and remove from fire.
13. Sprinkle tandoori masala or chaat masala. Toss for a minute. Serve hot.

Methi
(FENUGREEK)

Methi Paaro

Serves 3-4

250 gm fresh methi (fenugreek leaves)
2 tbsp fresh curd - beaten well with a fork till smooth
2 tbsp oil
½ tsp jeera (cumin seeds), 4-5 flakes garlic - chopped & crushed
3 onions - chopped
2 tsp ginger paste, 1 tomato - finely chopped
1 tsp salt, ½ tsp red chilli powder

1. Remove the hard stems from methi. Chop finely. Wash leaves nicely in 2-3 changes of water.
2. Heat oil. Add jeera. When it turns golden, add garlic.
3. When garlic changes colour, add onions. Stir fry till onions turn brown.
4. Add ginger paste and red chilli powder. Stir for a few seconds.
5. Add the tomatoes. Stir fry for 4-5 minutes.
6. Add methi. Bhuno for 10 minutes on medium flame. Add salt.
7. Add beaten curd. Mix well and serve hot.

Kasoori Methi Paneer

Serves 4

1 packet (25 gms) kasoori methi (dried fenugreek leaves)
3 tbsp oil (preferably mustard or any refined oil)
a tiny grain of hing (asafoetida)
1 cup milk
200 gms paneer- cut in tiny cubes
¼ tsp haldi, ½ tsp red chilli powder
2 pinches sugar, ½ tsp salt or to taste

1. Remove hard stems from kasoori methi. Soak in warm water for about 15 minutes.
2. Fry paneer cubes to a golden colour.
3. Heat mustard oil to smoking point. Remove from fire. Add hing.
4. Drain and squeeze the soaked methi and add to the oil. Return to fire. Stir fry on low flame for 4-5 minutes.
5. Add salt, sugar, haldi and chilli powder. Bhuno for a few seconds.
6. Add milk. Boil. Add fried paneer. Cook covered till milk is almost dry.

Fenugreek & Spinach Curry

The two greens blend wonderfully!

Serves 4

CURRY

250 gms paalak (spinach) - discard stalks and chop leaves
125 gms methi (fenugreek leaves) - discard stalks and chop leaves
2 tbsp desi ghee (clarified butter)
½ tsp haldi
1 tsp red chilli powder
½ tsp salt or to taste
2 tomatoes - chopped
3 tbsp dahi (yoghurt) - beaten well
1 tsp garam masala
1 tsp dhania (coriander) powder

OPTIONAL INGREDIENTS
4 medium potatoes - peeled and cut into 1" pieces
or
150 gms paneer - cut into 1" pieces

1. Heat ghee in a kadhai. Reduce flame. Add haldi and red chilli powder.
2. Add tomatoes. Stir fry till well blended & ghee separates.
3. Add spinach and fenugreek leaves. Add salt, cook for 5-7 minutes.
4. Add the yoghurt, garam masala, coriander powder. Stir till yoghurt gets well blended and turns dry.
5. Remove from heat and allow to cool. Blend to a thick puree.
6. Transfer the puree to the kadhai and add about 1 cup hot water to get a curry. Boil. Check salt. Simmer on low flame for a few minutes.
7. Eat this curry plain or add paneer pieces or fry potatoes on medium flame till they are crisp and golden brown, and add to the hot curry.

Khumb
(MUSHROOM)

Makki Matar Khumb

Mushrooms with corn and peas in a delicious fenugreek flavoured white gravy.

Serves 4-5   *Picture on page 49*

200 gms mushrooms - preferably small in size
¾ cup corn niblets (daane of 1 large bhutta or tinned corn kernels)
1 cup shelled, boiled or frozen peas
4 tbsp kasoori methi (dry fenugreek leaves)
1 tsp ginger-garlic paste, a pinch of pepper
1 tbsp butter, 3 tbsp oil
2 onions - ground to a paste
½ cup thin fresh cream or malai
1 tsp salt, or to taste, ½ tsp red chilli powder, ½ tsp garam masala
a pinch of amchoor
1 cup milk (approx.)

GRIND TOGETHER
½ stick dalchini (cinnamon), seeds of 2-3 chhoti illaichi (green cardamom)
3-4 laung (cloves), 4-5 saboot kali mirch (peppercorns)
2 tbsp cashewnuts (kaju)

1. Boil whole fresh corn or frozen corn kernels in 4 cups water with ¼ tsp haldi, 2 tsp sugar and 1 tsp salt to get soft, yellow, sweetish corn. If using tinned corn, simply drain the water and use.
2. Trim the stem of each mushroom. Leave them whole if small or cut them into 2 pieces, if big.
3. Heat 1 tbsp butter in a kadhai and add the mushrooms. Stir fry on high flame till dry and golden.
4. Add 1 tsp ginger-garlic paste, ½ tsp salt and a pinch of white or black pepper. Stir for 1 more minute and remove from fire. Keep cooked mushrooms aside.
5. Grind together dalchini, seeds of chhoti illaichi, laung, kali mirch and cashews to a powder in a small mixer grinder.
6. Heat 3 tbsp oil. Add onion paste and cook on low heat till oil separates. Do not let the onions turn brown.
7. Add the freshly ground masala-cashew powder. Cook for a few seconds.
8. Add the kasoori methi and cream or malai, cook on low heat for 2-3 minutes till malai dries up.
9. Add salt, red chilli powder, garam masala and amchoor. Stir for 1 minute.
10. Add the boiled corn, peas and mushrooms.
11. Add 1 cup milk to get a thick gravy.
12. Add ½ cup water if the gravy appears too thick. Boil for 2-3 minutes. Serve.

Khumb Nadiyaan Kinare

Mushrooms with peas and tomato pieces in masala.

Picture on facing page   Serves 4

200 gm mushrooms - each cut into 4" pieces
2 cups green peas - boiled with little sugar and salt
1 large tomato - finely chopped
1 large onion - finely chopped
1 large tomato - cut into 1" pieces
1 tsp salt
¼ tsp haldi
½ tsp garam masala
1 tsp dhania powder
½ tsp red chilli powder
2 tsp finely chopped ginger
1 green chilli - chopped
3-4 tbsp cream

1. Cut one tomato into 1" pieces and remove pulp and keep aside to be added at the end. Chop the second tomato finely and mix with the pulp of the first tomato.
2. Heat 3 tbsp oil. Add onions and stir fry till soft.
3. Add chopped tomato and the pulp of the first tomato. Stir for 2 minutes.
4. Add mushrooms, stir fry for a minute.
5. Reduce heat. Add salt, haldi, garam masala, dhania powder and red chilli powder. Cook for 5-7 minutes on low heat.
6. Add boiled peas, ginger and green chillies. Keep aside till serving time.
7. At the time of serving, heat the vegetable. Add 3-4 tbsp cream and tomato pieces. Stir for 2 minutes. Serve hot.

Baby Corn Bullets : Recipe on page 29, Khumb Nadiyann Kinare ➤

Bharwaan Khumb Curry

Red pomegranates and cheese stuffed in mushrooms and put in a cardamom flavoured yellow gravy!

Serves 6-8

300 gm mushrooms (15-18 good size pieces)
juice of ½ lemon, 2 tsp salt
1 cup red kandhari anaar ke dane (fresh pomegranate)

FILLING
50 gms mozzarella or pizza cheese - grated finely (½ cup)
3 tbsp anaar ke dane
¼ tsp black pepper, 2-3 big pinches of salt

GRAVY
3 onions, 1½" piece ginger, 3 dry red chillies
4 tbsp oil, 4-5 chhoti illaichi (green cardamoms) - pounded to open slightly
½ tsp garam masala, ½ tsp red chilli powder, ½ tsp haldi, 1 tsp dhania powder,
1½ tsp salt, or to taste
1 cup milk
1 tbsp finely chopped coriander & 1 tbsp cream- to garnish

1. Wash mushrooms and pull out the stalks. Hollow the mushrooms a little more with the help of a small scooper. Keep stalks aside.
2. Boil for 4-5 cups water with 2 tsp salt and juice of ½ lemon. Add the mushrooms. Boil for 2 minutes. Drain and refresh with cold water. Strain. Wipe to dry well.
3. Mix all ingredients of the filling and stuff each mushroom with it. Place the mushrooms in a hot oven at 200°C for 5-7 minutes till cheese melts and the filling holds on to mushrooms well. Remove from oven and keep aside.
4. To prepare the gravy, blend the anaar ke daane with 1½ cups water in a mixer blender. Strain to get juice.
5. Trim the left over mushroom stalks. Grind mushroom stalks with onions, ginger and dry red chillies to a fine paste.
6. Heat 4 tbsp oil in a heavy kadhai. Add chhoti illaichi. Wait for a minute.
7. Add the onion-mushroom paste. Cook on low flame for about 7-8 minutes till onions turn light brown.
8. Add masalas - garam masala, red chilli powder, haldi, dhania and salt.
9. Add anaar ka ras. Boil, simmer for 5 minutes. Add milk to the gravy. Boil. Simmer on low flame for 5 minutes. Keep aside.
10. To serve, boil gravy. Pour in a serving dish. Arrange mushrooms on it. Heat in a microwave or an oven. Serve immediately, sprinkled with cream and coriander.

Mushroom Taka-Tak

Mushrooms cooked on the tawa and flavoured with whole spices.

Serves 4

1 packet (200 gm) mushrooms
1 capsicum - cut into 1" pieces
1 tbsp lemon juice
2 tbsp maida
¾ tsp salt
2 big pinches of baking powder
4 tbsp oil
2 onions - chopped
1 tsp dhania powder
3-4 green chillies - slit, deseeded & chopped
2-3 dry or fresh red chillies
3 tbsp ready made tomato puree

KHUSHBOO MASALA *(grind together to a rough powder)*
3-4 chhoti illaichi (green cardamom)
1" stick dalchini
4-5 laung (cloves)
½ tsp ajwain

1. Wash mushrooms well. Divide into two pieces. Boil 4-5 cups water with 2 tsp salt and 1 tbsp lemon juice. Remove water from fire and add the mushrooms to it. Keep mushrooms soaked in this hot water for 15 minutes.
2. Grind the ingredients of the khushboo masala in a small grinder or on the chakla-belan to a rough powder.
3. Sift maida, salt and baking powder together.
4. Drain the mushrooms well. Wipe dry on a clean kitchen towel. Sprinkle maida on the mushrooms. Rub a little to coat the mushrooms with maida.
5. Heat 3 tbsp oil on the tawa or a non stick pan. Add half of the mushrooms and saute till golden on all sides. Shift to the sides of the tawa. Saute the other half and shift to the sides of the tawa.
6. Add onions and capsicum to the left over oil in the centre of the tawa. Saute till onions turn transparent. Add 1 tsp dhania powder, green and red chillies.
7. Add ¾ tsp salt or to taste. Add tomato puree. Mix well.
8. Mix in the mushrooms from the sides.
9. Add the khushboo masala. Bhuno for 1-2 minutes. Serve hot.

Mushroom Chettinad

A brown mushroom curry with the fiery flavours of the South!

Serves 4

200 gm mushrooms - trim stalk and cut each into 2 pieces
5-6 saboot kali mirch (peppercorns) - crushed coarsely (½ tsp)

MASALA
1 onion - chopped finely
3 tomatoes - chopped finely
1" piece ginger, 8-10 flakes garlic
1 tbsp khus khus (poppy seeds), 2 tbsp kaju (cashewnuts)
3 tbsp curry leaves
½ tsp haldi (turmeric powder), ½ tsp red chilli powder
juice of ½ lemon, 1 tsp salt, or to taste

ROAST SPICES TOGETHER
1 tbsp oil
½ cup freshly grated coconut - remove brown skin before grating
1 tsp saboot dhania(coriander seeds)
½ tsp jeera (cumin seeds)
1 tsp saunf (fennel), 3-4 whole dry red chillies
seeds of 3 chhoti illaichi (green cardamom), 2-3 laung (cloves)
1" dalchini (cinnamon)

1. Wash mushrooms and trim the stalks. Cut into 2 pieces.
2. Soak khus khus and kaju in ½ cup warm water for 15 minutes.
3. Heat 1 tbsp oil on a tawa and roast all spices together on low heat till fragrant, for about 2-3 minutes. Remove from tawa. Cool.
4. Grind the roasted spices to a very smooth paste with in a small spice grinder, along with ginger-garlic and the khus and cashews with water. Keep paste aside.
5. Heat 3 tbsp oil in a kadhai and stir fry onions till light golden.
6. Add curry leaves. Wait for a minute.
7. Add the above ground paste. Saute for 1 minute on low heat.
8. Add chopped tomatoes, haldi, salt and chilli powder. Cook for 5-7 minutes till the tomatoes get well blended and oil separates.
9. Add mushrooms and lemon juice. Stir fry for 5 minutes. Mix well.
10. Add 1¼ cups water and chopped coriander. Give one boil. Simmer on low heat for 4-5 minutes, stirring occasionally till thick gravy is ready.
11. Sprinkle crushed peppercorns. Remove from fire. Serve hot with steamed rice.

Baingan
(BRINJAL)

Baingan Ka Saalan

Brinjals in a tamarind gravy.

Serves 4

6 small brinjals - cut into 4 pieces lengthwise and sprinkled with salt
4-5 achaari hari or laal mirch (large green or red chillies), optional
a lemon sized ball of imli (tamarind)
5 tbsp oil
½ tsp mustard seeds, ½ tsp kalonji
3 onions - finely chopped
a few curry leaves
2 tbsp cashews - soaked in 4 tbsp milk and ground to a paste
2 tbsp fresh cream

GRIND TOGETHER TO A SMOOTH PASTE
2 tbsp til (sesame seeds)
1 tsp desiccated coconut (coconut powder)
6 flakes garlic , 1½" piece of ginger
2 tsp dhania (coriander) powder, ¼ tsp haldi (turmeric) powder
1 tsp jeera
1 tsp salt
1 tsp fresh lemon juice

1. Wash the tamarind and put in a bowl with 1½ cups hot water. Mash and leave it to soak for 10 minutes.
2. Grind the sesame seeds, coconut, ginger, garlic, coriander, turmeric, jeera powder, salt and lemon juice to a paste with a little water. Keep aside.
3. Pat dry the brinjals sprinkled with salt on a clean kitchen towel.
4. Heat 5-6 tbsp oil in pan. Reduce heat and fry the green chillies for 1½ minutes. Remove the chillies from the oil and keep aside. In the same oil, add the brinjals. Fry turning sides on medium heat till they change colour and turn brownish. Check with a knife and remove from oil when they turn soft.
5. Heat 2 tbsp oil in a kadhai. Add kalonji and mustard seeds. Wait for ½ minute till they crackle, add onions and curry leaves. Fry till onions turn golden brown.
6. Add the freshly ground spices and fry for 2 minutes.
7. Add cashew paste and stir to mix well.
8. Add 2 cups water and stir. Pour strained tamarind juice. Boil. Simmer for 7-8 minutes on low heat.
9. Add the green chillies and brinjals. Cook for 5 minutes on low heat.
10. Add cream and remove from fire. Serve with rice or chappati.

Hyderabadi Baingan

Small brinjals stuffed with sesame seeds (til) and fresh coconut and put in masala.

Serves 4

250 gms small baingan (5-6 pieces), 6-7 tbsp oil

FILLING
2 tbsp til (sesame seeds)
a small piece fresh coconut - remove the brown skin and grate finely (3-4 tbsp)
½ tsp salt, ½ tsp red chilli powder, ½ tsp amchoor powder , ¼ tsp sugar

MASALA GRAVY
2 onions, 1" piece ginger, 2 dry whole red chillies, 3 tomatoes - grind all together
1 tsp dhania powder, ½ tsp amchoor (dried mango powder)
1 tsp salt or to taste, ½ tsp garam masala
2 pinches sugar

TOPPING (OPTIONAL)
2 tbsp fresh cream, 2 tbsp boiled peas

1. Wash baingans. Make two cross cuts from the top, leaving the end part intact.
2. Mix all ingredients of the filling together.
3. Fill 2 tsp filing in each baingan.
4. Heat 6-7 tbsp oil. Put the baingans in the oil and cook for 3-4 minutes stirring occasionally. Cover and cook for another 15 minutes till soft. Gently keep turning the baingans occasionally till very soft. Pick up the brinjals and keep aside. Drain the excess oil from the kadhai and keep aside.
5. To prepare the masala, grind onions, ginger, red chillies and tomatoes together to a paste.
6. Heat 4 tbsp oil in a kadhai. Add the onion - tomato paste. Cook till almost dry.
7. Add dhania powder, amchoor, garam masala and salt. Cook on low flame till oil separates.
8. Add 1½ cups hot water to get a gravy. Simmer gravy for 5-7 minutes on low flame. Keep gravy aside.
9. To serve, heat baingans separately. Sprinkle 2 pinches sugar, ¼ tsp amchoor and ¼ tsp salt on the baingans while being heated.
10. Heat the gravy separately.
11. Pour the gravy in a low sided dish. Carefully pick up each hot baingan and arrange neatly over the gravy.
12. Put a few drops of cream or well beaten curd on the gravy (not on the baingans) and arrange few boiled peas over the drops of cream. Serve.

Chutney Waale Bharwaan Baingan

A dry dish of brinjals which are stuffed with a nutty coriander paste.

Picture on page 69　　　　　　　*Serves 6*

400 gm (12) small round brinjals
a pinch of hing (asafoetida)
3 dry, whole red chillies
¼ tsp methi dana (fenugreek seeds)
1 onion - finely sliced
¼ tsp salt, ¼ tsp garam masala, ¼ tsp haldi, ¼ tsp red chilli powder
juice of ½ lemon
4 tbsp oil

DRY ROAST TOGETHER
2 tsp til (sesame seeds)
2 tsp saboot dhania (coriander seeds)
½ tsp jeera (cumin seeds)
2 whole, dry red chillies

NUTTY CHUTNEY
½ cup fresh coriander leaves
3 tbsp roasted peanuts
1 tomato
¾ tsp salt, or to taste, ¼ tsp sugar, ¼ tsp amchoor
1" piece ginger, 5-6 flakes garlic
2 green chillies

1. Wash and slit brinjals in four, leaving the stem intact. The brinjals should be intact at the base.
2. Mix the freshly roasted masalas with the ingredients of the nutty chutney and grind together to a thick paste.
3. Fill the brinjals with this paste.
4. Heat oil in pressure cooker. Add the hing, whole red chillies and methi dana.
5. Add the sliced onion and fry till light golden.
6. Add salt, garam masala, haldi and red chilli powder.
7. Add the brinjals. Gently fry them on low flame for 3-4 minutes or till the skin changes colour.
8. Add ½ cup water. Scrape the masala sticking to the bottom of the cooker. Close the cooker and pressure cook to give 1 whistle. Keep on low heat for 3 minutes. Remove from fire.
9. Sprinkle the lemon juice over the brinjals. Serve hot.

Baingan Achaari

A semi dry brinjal dish with lots of tomatoes and pickle spices.

Serves 4　　　　　*Picture on page 107*

750 gms (7- 8) brinjals of long thin variety
½ kg tomatoes - chopped finely
2 tsp ginger or garlic paste
15- 20 curry leaves
½ tsp haldi
½ tsp red chilli powder
1 tbsp dhania powder
1 tsp salt, or to taste

COLLECT TOGETHER
a pinch of hing (asafoetida)
1 tsp saunf (fennel)
½ tsp kalonji (onion seeds)
½ tsp methi dana (fenugreek seeds)
1 tsp rai (mustard seeds)

1. Cut brinjals into half lengthwise and then into 1" pieces.
2. Deep fry brinjals till light brown.
3. Heat 2 tbsp oil and add ginger or garlic paste. Add curry patta and stir fry for a minutes.
4. Reduce heat. Add all collected ingredients together – hing, saunf, kalonji, methi dana and rai. Stir till methi dana turns brown.
5. Add haldi, red chilli powder, dhania powder and salt. Stir for 30 seconds.
6. Add chopped tomatoes and stir for about 7-8 minutes or till oil separates.
7. Add fried baingans. Sprinkle ¼ tsp salt and stir gently on slow fire for a few minutes till well mixed. Serve hot.

Aloo
(POTATO)

Chutney Waale Bharwaan Baingan : Recipe on page 66 ➤

Shahi Kaaju Aloo

Potatoes coated with curd and cashew masala flavoured with black cumin.

Serves 6

4 potatoes
2 tbsp cashew halves (kaju tudkra)
4 tbsp kaju (cashews) - soaked in ¼ cup water
1 tbsp chopped ginger
1 tsp chopped garlic
4 tbsp oil
1 tsp shah jeera (black cumin)
1 tej patta (bay leaf)
2 onions - chopped
¼ tsp haldi (turmeric)
½ tsp garam masala
1 tsp salt, or to taste
¼ cup yogurt - whisked to make it smooth
¼ cup milk mixed with ½ cup water
oil for frying

1. Wash potatoes and peel. Cut potatoes into 1" pieces.
2. Deep fry the potatoes on medium heat till well cooked and they turn to a deep golden brown. Check with a knife to see that they are done. Keep aside. Fry the cashew halves also to a nice golden colour in the same oil. Remove from oil and keep aside.
3. Grind soaked kaju, ginger and garlic to a paste in a small coffee or spice grinder. Keep cashew paste aside.
4. Heat 4 tbsp oil in a heavy bottomed kadhai. Add sah jeera and tej patta. Let jeera change colour.
5. Add onions and cook on low heat till onions turn soft but do not let them turn brown.
6. Add haldi, garam masala and salt. Stir to mix well.
7. Add cashew paste. Cook for 1 minute.
8. Add yogurt and stir fry till water evaporates. Cook till dry.
9. Add milk and about ½ cup water to get a gravy. Boil and simmer uncovered for just 2-3 minutes.
10. Add the fried potatoes to the gravy and simmer on low heat. Cook on low heat till the gravy gets thick and coats the potatoes.
11. Add the fried cashew halves. Mix well. Serve hot with rotis or paranthas.

Aloo Pasanda

Slices of potatoes sandwiched with paneer filling and put in a gravy.

Serves 6

2 large round potatoes - peeled, cut into paper thin round slices
3 tbsp maida, 4 tbsp water, ¼ tsp salt, ¼ tsp red chilli powder

FILLING
100 gms paneer - grated finely
8-10 kishmish - soaked in water and chopped, 5-6 kaju - chopped
¼ tsp salt, a pinch of red chilli powder, a pinch of pepper

GRAVY
3 onions, 3 tomatoes, 1" piece ginger, 5-6 flakes garlic, 1 dry red chilli
4 tbsp oil, 2 tej patta (bay leaf), 2-3 laung (cloves)
½ tsp red chilli powder, 1½ tsp dhania (coriander) powder
¼ tsp haldi, 1½ tsp salt or to taste, 2 tsp chilli-garlic tomato sauce

GARNISH
1" cube of paneer - to grate, 1 tbsp chopped coriander

1. Peel and cut into paper thin, round slices. Keep aside in salted water.
2. Mix grated paneer with all the ingredients of the filling lightly with a spoon. Do not mash the paneer.
3. Prepare a thick paste with 3 tbsp maida and 4 tbsp water to get a thick batter of a coating consistency. Add salt, red chilli powder and pepper.
4. Sandwich 1 tsp of filling between 2 slices of potatoes. Press well.
5. Heat oil for deep frying.
6. Dip, first the sides of the sandwiched potato slices in the maida batter and then the whole piece in the batter. Deep fry on low flame to a golden colour. See that the potatoes get cooked on frying. Keep aside.
7. To prepare the gravy, grind the onions, ginger, garlic, tomatoes and dry red chilli to a paste in a blender.
8. Heat 4 tbsp oil. Add tej patta. Add onion-tomato paste. Cook till paste turns dry.
9. Add haldi, dhania and red chilli powder. Add laung. Cook on slow flame for 2-3 minutes till oil separates.
10. Add 1½ cups water. Boil. Add salt and chilli garlic tomato sauce. Simmer on low flame for 5-7 minutes. Keep aside.
11. To serve, heat gravy. Gently add the fried, stuffed aloos. Simmer for a minute.
12. Garnish with chopped coriander and paneer grated directly on the vegetable in the dish.

Dum Aloo Chutney Wale

Whole potatoes simmered in a tangy mint flavoured gravy.

Serves 5-6

8 baby potatoes - keep whole or 3 potatoes - each cut into 4 pieces

CHUTNEY
1 cup chopped fresh coriander, ½ small raw mango or ½ tsp amchoor
½ cup poodina (mint)
½ tsp salt, ½ tsp sugar

GRAVY
4 tbsp oil
2 onions - ground to a paste
2 tsp ginger paste, 2 tsp garlic paste
1 tsp jeera (cumin) seeds
1 tsp red chilli powder
1 cup yoghurt - beat till smooth and mix with 1½ cups water
2 tbsp cashewnuts - ground to a paste with a little water
1 tomato - chopped finely
½ tsp garam masala
1 tsp salt, or to taste

1. Peel and wash potatoes. Heat oil in a kadhai and deep fry over low heat until cooked and light brown in colour. Keep aside.
2. For the chutney, put all ingredients in a blender and make a paste. Keep chutney aside.
3. Beat yoghurt in a bowl. Add cashew paste and 1½ cups water. Mix well.
4. Heat oil in a kadhai.
5. Add onion paste, stir over low heat until transparent. Do not brown the onions.
6. Add the ginger and garlic pastes and stir until the oil leaves the masala.
7. Add jeera, stir for a minute.
8. Add chutney and red chilli powder, stir for ½ minute.
9. Remove from fire. Then add yoghurt, cashews and water mix, stirring continuously on low heat till it comes to a boil.
10. Now add the fried potatoes and salt. Simmer uncovered for 5 minutes until the oil leaves the masala and the gravy turns thick.
11. Add tomatoes and garam masala, stir and bring to a boil. Serve.

Note: Do not cover the kadhai while cooking.

Dilruba Aloo Matar

Potatoes coated with sesame seeds and mixed with peas to create an exotic dry dish.

Picture on page 79　　　　　　*Serves 4*

4-5 small sized potatoes
2 tsp til (sesame seeds)
4 tbsp oil
½ tsp jeera (cumin seeds)
2 onions - cut into rings
1 tomato - pureed or 2 tbsp ready made tomato puree
8-10 cashewnuts (kaju)
10-15 kishmish - soaked in water for 10 minutes and drained
1 cup boiled or frozen peas
¾ tsp salt
½ tsp haldi
½ tsp garam masala, ½ tsp red chilli powder
¼ tsp amchoor
2 tbsp chopped coriander
2 green chillies - slit lengthways

1. Boil potatoes in salted water until just tender. They should feel soft when a knife is inserted. Do not over cook. Peel and cut each potato into 2 equal halves.
2. Dry-roast til on a tawa on low flame, until golden brown. Keep aside.
3. Heat oil. Add jeera. When it splutters and turns golden, add onions. Cook until onions turn golden.
4. Add kaju. Stir-fry till golden.
5. Add tomato puree and cook till dry.
6. Add salt, garam masala, red chilli powder, amchoor, haldi, green chillies and fresh coriander. Cook for 1 minute.
7. Add the potatoes. Bhuno gently for about 5 minutes, taking care not to stir too often as this might break the potatoes. While bhunoing the potatoes, keep them spaced out and not overlapping each other so that they turn crisp.
8. Sprinkle til, keeping aside some for garnishing. Mix gently so that the potatoes are well coated with the til seeds.
9. Add boiled peas and kishmish. Stir to mix well. Remove from fire.
10. Transfer to a serving dish. Sprinkle some more til on the aloos. Serve.

Phali

(BEANS)

Masala Beans

Serves 4

250 gm french beans - threaded & chopped
2 onions - ground to a paste
1" piece ginger - grated
3-4 flakes garlic - crushed
2 tsp dhania powder, 1 tsp salt, or to taste
½ tsp garam masala
½ tsp red chilli powder
¾ cup dahi (yoghurt) - beat till smooth
½ cup milk

1. Pressure cook beans with ¼ cup water and ½ tsp salt to give 1 whistle. Remove from fire and keep aside.
2. Heat 3 tbsp oil in a kadhai. Add onions. Stir fry on low flame till golden.
3. Add ginger and garlic. Mix. Reduce flame. Add dhania powder, garam masala, red chilli and ½ tsp salt. Stir fry till onions turn brown.
4. Add curd, stirring continuously, till the masala turns brown again and oil separates.
5. Add boiled beans. Bhuno for 2 minutes. Add milk. Cook on low flame till masala turns thick. Serve.

Phalli Tamatar aur Kairi

Serves 4   *Picture on page 117*

250 gm french beans - threaded & cut diagonally into ½" pieces
1 medium kairi (unripe mango) - peeled & cut into tiny cubes or matchsticks
½ tsp rai (mustard seeds), ½ tsp kalaunji (onion seeds)
2-3 whole, dried red chillies, 4-8 curry leaves
2 tbsp chopped fresh coriander, 3 tomatoes - cut into tiny pieces
1 tsp salt,1 tsp dhania powder, ½ tsp garam masala, ¼ tsp haldi

1. Thread beans. Cut into ½" slanting pieces. Boil in ½ cup water with ½ tsp salt, until just tender. Set aside.
2. Heat 3 tbsp oil. Reduce flame. Add rai and kalaunji. Reduce flame.
3. After ½ minute add the whole red chillies and curry leaves. Stir for a few seconds.
4. Add coriander, dhania powder, garam masala, haldi, salt and tomatoes. Stir-fry for about 2-3 minutes.
5. Add the diced mango and the green beans and stir for about 5-7 minutes.

Note: It is essential to buy raw green mango for this dish for its sour, sharp flavour.

Beans with Nuggets

Increase the protein content of the dish by combining the green vegetable with soya bean nuggets.

Serves 4

250 gm french beans
½ cup nutri nuggets - soaked in ½ cup hot milk mixed with ½ cup water for 1 hour
2 onions - cut into rings
1" piece ginger - cut into match sticks
3-4 flakes garlic - crushed
2 green chillies - deseeded & finely chopped
2 laung - crushed
2 tomatoes - finely chopped
1 tsp tomato ketchup
¾ tsp garam masala
¾ tsp amchoor
1 tsp dhania powder
1½ tsp salt or to taste
3 tbsp oil
chopped coriander to garnish

1. Wash and soak nutri nuggets in hot milk and water mixture.
2. Thread beans. Cut into small pieces.
3. Heat oil in a kadhai. Add onions and stir fry till transparent.
4. Add ginger, garlic, green chillies and laung. Stir fry for 1 minute.
5. Add tomatoes. Stir fry till dry.
6. Reduce flame. Add tomato ketchup, garam masala, amchoor, dhania powder and salt. Cook for 2 minutes.
7. Add beans and bhuno for 5 minutes on medium flame.
8. Add nuggets along with the milk. Mix well. Give it 1-2 boils.
9. Cover and cook for 6-8 minutes, till the beans turn soft.
10. Uncover and bhuno for 5-7 minutes on low flame.
11. Serve hot garnished with chopped coriander and ginger match sticks.

Hari Gobhi
(BROCCOLI)

Broccoli Tandoori

Broccoli florets with long stalks are flavoured with carom seeds and barbecued.

Serves 4

2 small broccoli - cut into medium sized florets with long stalks
2 tsp salt
1 tsp sugar

1ST MARINADE
juice of 1 lemon (3-4 tsp)
¾ tsp carom seeds (ajwain)
1 tsp salt
½ tsp red chilli powder

2ND MARINADE
1 cup thick yogurt - hang for 20 minutes in a muslin cloth
½ cup thick cream
2 tsp ginger paste
½ tsp ajwain
½ tsp red chilli paste, optional
¾ tsp salt
1 tsp tandoori masala or chaat masala

1. Boil 5-6 cups of water in a large pan. Add 2 tsp salt and 1 tsp sugar to the water. Add broccoli pieces to the boiling water. Boil. Keep on boiling for 2 minutes. Drain. Refresh in cold water. Wipe broccoli well with a clean kitchen towel.

2. Spread the broccoli on a flat plate and sprinkle the ingredients of the 1st marinade. Marinate the broccoli for 15 minutes.

3. Drain the broccoli of any excess liquid.

4. Mix all the ingredients of the 2nd marinade. Check salt and add more if needed. Add the broccoli to it and mix well. Insert the marinate in between the florets of the broccoli, especially from the backside. Keep in the refrigerator till the time of serving.

5. Brush the grill of the oven or gas tandoor with some oil. Place the broccoli spears on it and barbecue them in a gas oven for 10 minutes or grill in a preheated electric oven at 210°C/410°F for 5 minutes. Baste(pour on the broccoli) with some oil in between and grill further for 5 minutes. Do not over grill it, it turns too dry. Serve hot as a side dish.

Makhani Mirch Makai : Recipe on page 28 ➤
Dilruba Aloo Matar : Recipe on page 73 ➤

Hari Gobhi Besani Tukri

Whole broccoli, batter fried and served in the tandoori style.

Picture on page 2   *Serves 4*

1 whole broccoli flower

MARINADE
2 tbsp lemon juice
1 tsp salt
½ tsp red chilli powder
½ tsp ajwain (carom seeds)
1 tbsp ginger paste

BATTER
½ cup besan (gram flour)
¼ cup milk, approx.
1 tsp ginger paste
½ tsp ajwain
1 tbsp chopped coriander
½ tsp salt, ¼ tsp red chilli powder, ¼ tsp garam masala

SALAD
1 tomato - cut into four pieces, a few kheera slices and some onion rings

TO SPRINKLE
some chat masala

1. Remove stem of broccoli. Boil 8 cups water with 2 tsp salt and 1 tsp sugar. Put the whole broccoli in it. Put the broccoli with stem side down. See that the whole broccoli is dipped in water. Bring to a boil again. Boil for 3-4 minutes till the stalks turn soft. Check with a knife. Remove from fire. Remove from water and refresh in cold water. Wipe dry with a clean kitchen towel.

2. Mix all ingredients of the marinade. Insert the marinate in between the florets of the broccoli, especially from the backside. Keep aside for 15 minutes.

3. Mix all ingredients of the batter in a deep big bowl. Add enough milk to get a thick coating batter.

4. Heat oil for deep frying in a kadhai. Dip the broccoli in the batter. Spread the left over batter nicely with the hands on the broccoli to cover nicely.

5. Carefully put in hot oil and deep fry till golden on medium heat. Remove from fire. Cut into four pieces.

6. Sprinkle some chaat masala on the broccoli. Serve immediately along with salad sprinkled with some chaat masala.

Cheesy Broccoli Koftas

Serves 4-6   *Picture on page 2*

1 medium broccoli - grated finely along with tender stalks (2 cups grated)
1 potato - boiled and grated
2 tbsp roasted peanuts - crushed coarsely
¼ tsp coarsely crushed saboot kali mirch (peppercorns)
½ tsp salt, ¼ tsp garam masala, ¼ tsp amchoor
1½ tbsp cornflour, a pinch of baking powder
1 cheese cube (20 gm) - cut into 10 pieces, ½ tbsp butter

GRAVY
2 onions and 1" piece ginger - ground to a paste
2 tbsp cashewnuts and 2 tbsp magaz(watermelon seeds) - soaked in ½ cup hot water for 5 minutes or use 4 tbsp of kaju (cashews)
4 tbsp dahi (yogurt), 3 tbsp oil
1 tsp kasoori methi, 1 tsp garam masala, ½ tsp chilli powder, 1¼ tsp salt, or to taste
½ cup cream mixed with ½ cup milk
seeds of 3 chhoti illaichi (green cardamoms) - crushed

1. Grate the broccoli florets and the tender stems very finely.
2. Heat butter in a pan. Add chopped broccoli. Add ¼ tsp salt. Stir on medium heat for 3-4 minutes on low heat. Remove from heat.
3. Grate the potato well. Add peanuts, salt, crushed peppercorns, garam masala, amchoor, cornflour, baking powder and cooked broccoli to the potato.
4. Make balls of the potato-broccoli mixture.
5. Flatten a ball and put a small piece of cheese in it. Make a ball again.
6. Deep fry 2-3 balls at a time till golden. Drain on absorbent paper.
7. For gravy, drain cashewnuts and magaz, grind them along with curd to a paste.
8. Heat 3 tbsp oil. Add onion and ginger paste. Stir fry onion paste on low flame till oil separates and it turns transparent. Do not let it turn brown.
9. Gradually add curd-cashewnut mixture, stirring continuously. Bhuno for 4-5 minutes till masala turns thick and oil separates.
10. Add kasoori methi, garam masala, red chilli and salt. Stir for 1-2 minutes.
11. Reduce heat. Add cream mixed with milk. Stir to mix well.
12. Add 2 cups water. Boil. Simmer for 2-3 minutes, on low flame, stirring constantly. Remove from fire and keep aside till serving time.
13. At serving time, add enough water (½-1 cup) to get a thin gravy. Add koftas. Keep on low heat & stir continuously till it boils. Keep on low heat for 2-3 minutes till koftas turn soft. Serve hot, sprinkled with grated cheese and coriander.

Jeera Broccoli

A quick and delicious hari subzi.

Serves 4

250 gm (1 small head) broccoli - cut into medium sized florets
3 tbsp oil
1 tsp jeera (cumin seeds)
2 onions - cut into rings
a thin slice of ginger - cut into match sticks (1 tbsp)
2 fresh red or green chillies - deseeded & cut into long pieces
2 tomatoes - chopped finely
½ tsp haldi
1 tsp salt
1 tsp dhania powder
½ tsp garam masala
½ tsp red chilli powder
½ tsp amchoor
2-3 green chillies
¼ cup milk

1. Heat oil in a kadhai. Reduce heat. Add jeera. Wait till golden.
2. Add onion, ginger and green chillies. Cook till onions start turning brown.
3. Add haldi and salt. Mix.
4. Add tomatoes and bhuno for 3-4 minutes.
5. Add dhania powder, garam masala, red chilli powder and amchoor. Mix for 1 minute.
6. Add broccoli. Stir fry for 2-3 minutes without covering. Cover and cook on low heat for 8-10 minutes or till done.
7. Add whole green chillies. Stir fry without covering for 2-3 minutes.
8. Remove from fire. Immediately add milk and mix well. Serve hot.

Patta Gobhi

(CABBAGE)

Stuffed Cabbage Rolls

A very unusual baked dish. Whole cabbage leaves are filled with cottage cheese filling, placed on a bed of sweet and sour sauce and baked. This combination makes this dish really amazing! Must give it a try.

Picture on back cover   Serves 6-8

8 outer large cabbage leaves
FILLING
2 onions - chopped
1½ cups paneer - crumbled (200 gm)
1½ cups tomato puree
1 tsp vinegar
2 flakes garlic - crushed
4 tbsp oil
1 tsp sugar
¼ tsp haldi
¾ tsp salt
½ tsp pepper

1. To break the outer leaves, cut leaves from the stalk end and gently pull from the cut end to get a whole leaf.
2. Boil 6-7 cups of water in a large pan with 2 tsp of salt and 1 tsp sugar. Add cabbage leaves to the boiling water. Cook cabbage in boiling salted water for atleast 3-4 minutes till soft. Hard leaves do not taste good! Drain and cool.
3. Heat 2 tbsp oil. Add onion and cook till golden.
4. Add haldi and the paneer. Mix well. Add ½ tsp salt & ¼ tsp pepper to taste. Stir for 1 minute and remove from fire.
4. To make the sauce, heat 2 tbsp oil and fry the garlic till it just changes colour. Add the tomato puree, vinegar, sugar, ¾ tsp salt and ½ tsp pepper. Cook for 2 minutes. Remove from fire and check seasonings. Keep aside.
5. Spread a cabbage leaf on a flat surface. Cut off the hard end portion of the leaf.
6. Divide the paneer mixture into 8 portions. Place one portion of paneer in the centre of a cabbage leaf. Spread it along the width of the leaf and then roll. Pierce a toothpick on the hard central vein of the leaf.
7. Spread 3-4 tbsp sauce at the bottom of a greased baking dish.
8. Place the rolls close together in the baking dish.
9. Spread the left over sauce on the cabbage rolls.
10. Cover with aluminium foil and bake in a preheated oven at 180°C/350°F/Gas mark 4 for 20 minutes.

Khatti Meethi Patta Gobhi

A different style of making cabbage in which the red sauce has carrot also in it. Tastes good with steamed rice.

Serves 6

1 medium cabbage (about 750 gm) - cut into 1" squares
4 large tomatoes - chopped
½ cup grated carrot (1 big)
4 tbsp oil
2 tbsp cornflour dissolved in 1 cup water
1 tbsp vinegar
1 tbsp soya sauce
1½ tbsp tomato ketchup
1 tsp salt, or to taste

1. Put tomatoes in boiling water for 3-4 minutes. Remove from water and remove the skin and chop.
2. Cut cabbage into 1" squares. Saute in 2 tbsp butter in a kadhai for 3-4 minutes till brown specs appear. Add ¼ tsp salt and ¼ tsp pepper. Mix and remove from kadhai.
3. Heat 2 tbsp oil in the same kadhai and fry the grated carrot & chopped tomatoes for about 5 minutes.
4. Remove carrot- tomatoe mixture from fire. Cool. Blend in a mixer.
5. Return to fire the pureed tomatoes and cook till the mixture is thick
6. Mix cornflour in 1 cup of water in a bowl. Add vinegar, sugar, soya sauce and salt and mix well.
7.   Add to the tomatoes and cook till it turns saucy.
8. Add the cabbage to the tomato sauce. Mix gently. Add a pinch of sugar if you like. Serve.

Patta Gobhi aur Pyaaz ki Bhujia

The onion and mustard seeds make this dry side dish very appetizing.

Serves 4

1 small cabbage - chopped
½ tsp kalaunji (onion seeds)
1 tsp rai (mustard seeds)
a few curry leaves
3 dry, whole red chillies
2 onions - sliced
1" piece ginger - cut into thin match sticks (shredded)
2 tomatoes - finely chopped
1 tsp salt
½ tsp haldi
½ tsp chilli powder
½ tsp garam masala
juice of ½ lemon

1. Heat 3 tbsp oil in a big kadhai. Add kalaunji and rai. Reduce flame.
2. After ½ minute, add curry leaves and whole red chillies. Stir.
3. Add the sliced onions. Stir fry until light brown. Add ginger.
4. Add tomatoes. Stir fry for 3-4 minutes.
5. Add salt, haldi, red chilli and garam masala. Stir-fry for 1 minute.
6. Add cabbage and cook uncovered, stirring occasionally, for about 10 minutes till the cabbage is cooked.
7. Add lemon juice. Mix well. Serve.

Cabbage Peanut Poriyal

A dry, spicy and crunchy South Indian side dish.

Serves 4   *Picture on page 89*

½ kg cabbage (1 medium) - chopped finely
½ cup peanuts - roasted
1½ tsp salt, or to taste

TEMPERING (CHOWNK)
4 tbsp oil
1 tsp rai (mustard seeds)
½ tsp jeera (cumin seeds)
2 tsp urad dal (split black gram)
2 tsp channa dal (bengal gram dal)
2 red chilli - broken into bits
½ tsp hing (asafoetida)
¼ cup curry leaves

PASTE (GRIND TOGETHER)
2 green chillies
4-5 tbsp grated coconut - remove the brown skin and then grate
1 onion - chopped
1 tsp jeera
2 tbsp curd

1.   Heat oil. Reduce heat. Add all ingredients of tempering.
2.   When dals turn golden, add the chopped cabbage.
3.   Add salt and 2 tbsp water.
4.   Add peanuts. Cover & cook on low heat for 7-8 minutes till cabbage turns tender.
5.   Add the coconut paste. Stir fry for 3-4 minutes. Serve hot.

Note: You can make any poriyal in the same way - carrot, beetroot or capsicum.

Hara Chholia
(FRESH GREEN GRAM)

Cabbage Peanut Poriyal : Recipe on page 87 ➢
Aloo Bhare Karele : Recipe on page 98 ➢

Chholia-Nugget Currry

Serves 6

1½ cups hare chane or chholia (fresh green gram)
5-6 pieces of nutri nuggets - soaked in hot milk for 1 hour - optional

FLAVOURING PASTE
½ tbsp oil
1 tbsp khus khus (poppy seeds)
3 chhoti illaichi (green cardamom)
2" piece dry coconut or 1 tbsp desiccated (powder) coconut
3-4 laung (cloves), 1 tej patta
a blade of javitri (mace)

OTHER INGREDIENTS
3 onions, ½" piece ginger
2 tomatoes
2 tsp dhania (coriander) powder
½ cup dahi - well beaten
1½ tsp salt or to taste, 1 tsp red chilli powder, ½ tsp garam masala
4 tbsp oil

1. To prepare the flavouring paste, collect together - khus khus, chhoti illaichi, dry coconut, laung, tej patta and javitri.
2. Heat ½ tbsp oil in a small heavy bottomed pan or on a tawa. Reduce flame. Add the collected spices of the flavouring paste together and fry on very low flame till khus khus turns golden. Remove tej patta.
3. Grind fried spices together to a rich aromatic paste with ¼ cup water in a grinder. Keep paste aside.
4. Also seperately grind onions, tomatoes and ginger to a paste in a grinder.
5. Heat 4 tbsp oil. Add dhania powder. Cook for ½ minute.
    Add the onion-tomato paste. Cook till oil separates. Reduce flame.
6. Add garam masala, red chilli powder and salt. Cook for ½ minute.
7. Beat curd with a fork and add to the onion masala. Cook, stirring till the masala turns brown again and oil separates.
8. Add the left over milk of the nutri nuggets. Cook till dry.
9. Add washed hare chane and the soaked nutri nuggets. Cook on low flame for 4-5 minutes.
10. Add 2 cups water. Boil. Cook on low flame till the hara channas get cooked.
11. Add the flavouring paste to the hare chane ki curry. Cook on low flame for 5 minutes. Serve hot.

Hare Channe ki Subzi

A dry preparation of fresh green gram with onion rings.

Serves 3-4

150 gm green chholia (fresh green gram)
3 tbsp oil
3 onions - cut into rings
1 tsp grated ginger
½ tsp jeera (cumin seeds)
1 cup chopped fresh coriander
¼ tsp haldi
½ tsp red chilli
½ tsp garam masala
1 tsp dhania powder
½ tsp salt or to taste
1 tomato - cut into ½" pieces
few drops of lemon juice

1. Heat 1 tbsp oil. Add washed chholia and ¼ tsp salt. Cover and cook for about 5-7 minutes, till done. Remove from fire and keep aside.
2. In a clean kadhai heat 2 tbsp oil. Reduce flame. Add jeera. Wait till it turns golden.
3. Add onion rings and ginger. Stir fry till onions turn transparent.
4. Add the powdered masalas and ½ tsp salt.
5. Add 1 cup chopped coriander and tomato. Mix well.
6. Add the cooked chholia and lemon juice. Mix well. Serve hot.

Chholia Paneer Curry

A red curry flavoured with whole spices. You may use potatoes instead of paneer.

Serves 5-6

200 gm chholia (green gram)
100 gms paneer (cottage cheese) - cut into 1" cubes & deep fried
4 - 5 tbsp oil
2 moti illaichi (black cardamom)
2 laung (cloves)
1" stick dalchini (cinnamon)
3 tomatoes - pureed
½ tsp haldi
¼ tsp amchoor
¾ tsp red chilli powder
2 tsp dhania powder
¾ tsp garam masala
1½ tsp salt or to taste
2 tbsp chopped coriander
1 tsp tandoori masala or barbecue masala

PASTE
3 onions
1" piece ginger & 4-6 flakes garlic - crushed to a paste

1. Deep fry big paneer pieces to a nice reddish brown colour. Keep aside.
2. To prepare gravy, grind onions to a paste in a grinder. Grind tomatoes separately.
3. Crush ginger and garlic to a rough paste.
4. Heat oil in a kadhai. Add 2 moti illaichi (black cardamom), 2 laung (cloves), 1" stick dalchini (cinnamon). Wait for a minute.
5. Add onion- ginger garlic paste. Fry onion paste in oil till light brown.
6. Add haldi, amchoor, red chilli powder, dhania powder, garam masala and salt. Cook on low flame till onions turn brown.
7. Add fresh tomato puree. Cook till dry. Bhuno the masala for about 7-8 minutes on low flame. Bhuno till oil separates.
8. Add chholia. Bhuno for 5-7 minutes. Add 2½ cups water.
9. Transfer the vegetable to a pressure cooker. Add fried paneer.
10. Close the pressure cooker and give one whistle. Keep on low flame for 2 minutes. Remove from fire.
11. After the pressure drops, add tandoori masala. Mix well.
12. Serve garnished with chopped coriander.

Bhein

(LOTUS STEM)

Peshawari Bhein

An unusual style to make crunchy lotus stem.

Serves 4

250 gm bhein or kamal kakri (lotus stem), choose thick ones
1" piece ginger
4-5 flakes garlic
2 green chillies
½ tsp ajwain (carom seeds)
1 tsp lemon juice
1 tbsp curd
¾ tsp salt
½ tsp red chilli powder
5-6 tbsp oil
2 tbsp atta (wheat flour)

1. Choose thick lotus stem (bhein). Cut bhein diagonally into ½" thick, slanting pieces. Wash well. Use a toothpick to clean if it is dirty. Boil in salted water till soft; or pressure cook in 1 cup water to give one whistle. Keep on low flame for 8-10 minutes.
2. Grind ginger, garlic, green chillies and ajwain to a paste.
3. Add lemon juice, curd, salt and red chilli powder to the above paste. Mix well.
4. Strain the boiled bhein. Dry them on a clean kitchen towel.
5. Apply the paste all over on the bhein. Keep aside for 1 hour.
6. At serving time, heat 5-6 tbsp oil. Reduce flame. Add atta. Cook for ½ - 1 minute till the atta turns golden brown.
7. Add the marinated (rubbed with paste) bhein and stir fry for 5-6 minutes on low flame till the atta coats the bhein.
8. Sprinkle some amchoor powder and garam masala. Stir fry for 2-3 minutes till they turn dry and crisp. Serve.

Note: At the time of buying bhein, see that both the **ends** are **closed.** The closed ends prevent the dirt from going inside.
Do not buy very thin bhein.

Punjabi Bhein Masala

Stuffed pieces of lotus stem, coated with flour.

Serves 4

300 gm (2 medium) bhein or kamal kakri (lotus stem), thick pieces
4 tbsp oil
2 tbsp atta (whole wheat flour)

FILLING (MIX TOGETHER)
2" piece ginger - crushed to a paste,   8-10 flakes garlic - crushed to a paste
1 tsp salt
½ tsp red chilli powder
½ tsp haldi
½ tsp amchoor
1½ tsp dhania powder
¾ tsp garam masala
1 tsp oil

1. Peel bhein. Cut into 1½" long pieces.
2. Put bhein in a pressure cooker with 1 cup water and ½ tsp salt. Keep on fire to give 1 whistle and then reduce heat and keep for 7-8 minutes on low heat. Remove from fire and keep aside.
3. Mix all ingredients of the filling together.
4. Make a slit in each boiled piece of bhein and fill the stuffing with the knife as you keep making the slit. Fill all the pieces and keep the left over filling aside.
5. Heat 4 tbsp oil in a large kadhai. Add 2 tbsp atta. Bhuno for 2 minutes on low heat.
6. Add the left over ginger-garlic filling and bhuno for a few seconds.
7. Add the bhein and stir fry for 5-7 minutes on medium flame till well browned. While bhunoing the bhein, spread out the vegetable in the kadhai so that all the pieces get well browned and turn crisp. Do not collect them in the centre of the kadhai.
8. Add fresh coriander and mix well. Serve hot with paranthas.

Safed Jalpari

The water vegetable - lotus stem is coated with a white yogurt paste and stir fried to a delicious dry dish.

Picture on page 127 **Serves 4**

300 gm (2 medium) bhein or kamal kakri (lotus stem)-cut into diagonal thick pieces
3 onions - each cut into 4 pieces and separated
2 tbsp oil
1 tsp ajwain (carom seeds)
¼ tsp haldi
¼ tsp salt, ¼ tsp red chilli powder
2-3 tbsp chopped coriander

MARINADE
1½ cups curd - hang for ½ hour
1 tsp ajwain (carom seeds)
1 tbsp finely chopped coriander
1½ tbsp besan (gram flour)
1 tbsp ginger garlic paste
1 tbsp oil
1 tsp salt
½ tsp red chilli powder
½ tsp haldi
1½ tsp dhania powder
½ tsp garam masala

TO SERVE
some chaat masala

1. Peel bhein. Cut into diagonal pieces of 1½" thickness.
2. Put bhein in a pan with 3-4 cups water and 1 tsp salt. Keep on fire. Boil. Reduce heat and cook covered for about 10 minutes on low heat. Remove from fire. Cut into 2 pieces lengthwise.
3. Mix all ingredients of the marinade together.
4. Add the boiled pieces of bhein to the marinade. Mix well to coat nicely.
5. Heat 2 tbsp oil in a kadhai. Add ajwain and wait till golden.
6. Add onions. Stir till golden.
7. Add haldi, salt and red chilli powder. Mix.
8. Add the marinated bhein along with all the marinade. Cook on low heat, keeping the vegetable spread out. Cook covered till bhein turns golden.
9. Add the coriander and mix well. Serve sprinkled with chaat masala.

Karela

(BITTER GOURD)

Aloo Bhare Karele

Stuffed bitter gourds. A few raisins are added to overcome the bitterness of the gourds.

Picture on page 89   *Serves 6-8*

500 gm (8 - 9) medium bitter gourds (karelas)

FILLING
2 large potatoes - boiled & mashed coarsely
½ tsp jeera (cumin seeds)
½ tsp sarson (mustard seeds)
1 onion - sliced finely
¼ tsp haldi powder
½ tsp chilli powder, salt to taste
¾ tsp garam masala
1½ tbsp kishmish (raisins) - soaked in water for 15 minutes
1 tsp til - roasted on a tawa (gridle) for a minute
1 tomato - chopped
2 green chillies - deseeded & chopped
2 - 3 tbsp chopped coriander
1 tsp amchoor

1. Peel karelas, keeping the stalks intact. Slit. Remove all seeds if they are hard, if not too hard, remove some to make place for the stuffing. Rub salt inside and on the surface of karelas. Keep aside for at least 1 hour.
2. Heat 3 tbsp oil in a kadhai. Reduce flame. Add jeera and sarson. Fry till jeera changes colour.
3. Add onions and fry till transparent. Add salt, red chilli powder, garam masala and haldi powder.
4. Add kishmish and til. Mix.
5. Add tomato, green chillies and coriander. Stir fry for 1- 2 minutes.
6. Add the roughly mashed potatoes and amchoor. Bhuno for 4-5 minutes on low flame. Remove from fire.
7. Squeeze the karelas, wash a few times.
8. Fill 1-2 tbsp of potato stuffing in each karela. Press to join the sides.
9. Heat 4-5 tbsp oil in a big flat bottomed kadhai. Put in the karelas, one by one gently. Cook uncovered on medium flame for 10-12 minutes, turning them occasionally, to brown them evenly. Cover and cook further for 5 minutes or till soft.
10. Remove from fire & drain out the extra oil. Serve sprinkled with some roasted til.

Saunfiyan Karela Subzi

Round slices of bitter gourd in a fennel flavoured masala.

Serves 4

**350 gm (7 medium) karelas (bitter gourd) - peeled, cut into slices, rubbed with
2 tbsp vinegar and 1 tsp salt & kept away for ½ hour atleast
¾ tsp saunf (fennel)
3 onions - sliced
1 green chilli - deseeded and chopped
1" piece ginger - chopped
3 tomatoes - chopped
2 tsp dhania powder
½ tsp garam masala
¾ tsp salt
¾ tsp red chilli powder
oil to deep fry**

1. Peel karelas. Cut them into round slices. Do not make the slices too thin as they turn too crisp on frying if very thin.
2. Sprinkle 2 tbsp vinegar and 1 tsp salt on them. Rub well. Keep aside for atleast ½ hour.
3. Wash well. Squeeze. Wash 2-3 times. Squeeze well to drain out all the bitterness alongwith water.
4. Heat some oil in a kadhai. Add the squeezed karelas and fry till golden brown. Drain and keep aside.
5. Heat 2 tbsp oil. Add saunf. When it changes colour, add the onions. Stir fry till light brown.
6. Add ginger and green chillies. Mix well.
7. Add tomatoes. Stir fry for 2-3 minutes till they turn soft.
8. Add dhania powder, garam masala, salt and red chilli powder. Stir for 2 minutes.
9. Add the fried karelas. Stir fry for 1-2 minutes.
10. Add more vinegar (1-2 tsp) to taste. Cook further for a few minutes. Serve hot with chappatis.

Note: Sirka (vinegar) removes the bitterness of the karelas and also adds taste to them.

Bharwaan Karele

Serves 4-6

½ kg small karelas (bitter gourd) - peeled, slit & deseeded
1 tsp salt
2 tbsp (a lemon sized ball) imli (tamarind)
3 tbsp plus 3 tbsp (6 tbsp) oil
1 tsp saunf and 1 tsp jeera - crushed slightly on a chakla-belan
¼ tsp kalonji (onion seeds)
¼ tsp methi daana (fenugreek seeds)
¼ tsp sarson
3 onions - grated or chopped very finely
6-8 flakes garlic - crushed
2 green chillies - deseeded & chopped
½ tsp salt
½ tsp chilli powder
2 tsp dhania (coriander) powder
¼ tsp haldi
1 small kairi (raw mango) - peeled & grated (¼ cup) or 1 tsp amchoor
6-8 small baby onions - peel and give 2 cross slits
some chaat masala

1. Boil 4 cups water with 1 tsp salt and imli. Add peeled and deseeded karelas. Boil on medium heat for 7-10 minutes or till soft. Strain. Keep aside.
2. Collect seeds - saunf, jeera, kalonji, methi daana and sarson together.
3. Heat 3 tbsp oil in a pan. Add the collected seeds and stir for a few seconds till methi daana turns golden brown.
4. Add onion and cook till light pink in colour. Add garlic and green chillies. Cook further for ½ minute.
5. Add salt, red chilli powder, haldi and dhania powder. Add the raw mango or amchoor and cook till dry. Remove from heat and keep the filling aside to cool.
6. Fill the boiled karela with the prepared onion mixture.
7. Heat the remaining 3 tbsp oil in a big, heavy bottomed pan or kadhai. Place each karela carefully in oil. Turn a little to coat with oil. Then shift to the side. Add all the karelas. Keep them side by side and not overlapping each other. Cook on low heat for 10-15 minutes stirring in-between till karelas turn golden brown on all sides.
8. Add whole onions and cook further for 5 minutes. Sprinkle chaat masala. Remove from fire and serve hot.

Tinda, Parwal
(Small Gourds)

Bharwaan Parwal

Parwals stuffed with paneer and potato filling!

Serves 4

250 gm (8 medium parwal)

MARINATION
1 tbsp lemon juice
½ tsp red chilli powder
½ tsp haldi, ½ tsp salt

FILLING
50 gm paneer - grated (½ cup)
1 small potato - boiled and cut into tiny cubes
½" piece ginger - chopped finely
1 tsp hara dhania (fresh coriander) - chopped
½ tsp amchoor (mango powder)
¼ tsp garam masala, ¼ tsp kala namak
a few cashewnuts - chopped, a few kishmish, salt to taste

GRAVY
1 tbsp desi ghee/2 tbsp oil
½ tsp jeera (cumin seeds)
a pinch hing (asafoetida)
¾ cup dahi - well beaten
2½ tsp dhania (coriander) powder
½ tsp red chilli powder, salt to taste
½ tsp haldi
1 tomato - pureed in a mixer
½ tsp garam masala
1 tbsp roasted cashewnuts - ground to a powder
1 cup water
¾ tsp salt or to taste

GARNISH
grated paneer, toasted almonds, tomato dices

1. Wash, peel, slit each parwal. Scoop out a little and remove seeds.
2. Mix all the ingredients of the marinade and rub the parwal - inside and out, with this marinade. Keep aside for 15 minutes.
3. Heat oil in kadhai and deep fry the marinated parwal over medium heat for 5-7 minutes or until cooked. Remove on absorbent paper to drain the excess oil.

4. Mix all the ingredients of the filling with the paneer and potato and divide them into 8 equal portions.
5. Stuff a portion of the filling in each parwal, pressing to ensure it is firmly packed. Keep aside.
6. To prepare the gravy, soak hing in 1 tbsp of water.
7. Beat dahi in a bowl, and mix dhania powder, red chilli and haldi powder.
8. Heat ghee/oil in a handi or kadhai, add cumin seeds, stir over medium heat until they begin to pop. Add hing, stir for few seconds.
9. Remove handi from heat and stir in the dahi mixture, return handi to heat and bhuno until dry and the ghee leaves the sides.
10. Add the tomato puree, bhuno until the ghee/oil leaves the sides.
11. Add cashewnut powder and bhuno for a minute.
12. Add water, bring to a boil, reduce to low heat, simmer, stirring occasionally, until the water is reduced slightly.
13. Add the stuffed parwal and simmer, stirring occasionally and carefully, for 5-6 minutes or until the gravy is of medium thick consistency.
14. Remove the parwal to a serving dish, pour on the gravy, garnish with grated paneer, toasted almonds and tiny tomato pieces. Serve with poori or phulka.

Hari Dahi Mein Parwal

Serves 4   *Picture on page 107*

250 gm tender parwals - scraped lightly with a knife & slit
2 tsp saunf and 1 onion - ground together roughly
2 tsp dhania powder, ½ tsp red chilli, ½ tsp garam masala, ½ tsp amchoor
½ tsp jeera, 2 whole, dry red chillies

GRIND TOGETHER
1 cup curd, 1"piece ginger, 1 green chilli and ½ cup fresh coriander, ¼ tsp salt

1. Heat 1 tbsp oil. Add saunf and onion paste. Cook till onions turn light brown. Add dhania powder, red chilli powder, garam masala, amchoor and ¼ tsp salt. Mix well and remove from fire. Fill the onion mixture into the parwals.
2. Grind coriander, ginger, green chilli, curd & salt to a green paste. Keep aside.
3. Heat 1½ tbsp oil in kadhai and stir fry stuffed parwals for 3 minutes. Sprinkle ½ tsp salt. Cover and cook on low flame till done. Transfer to a serving dish.
4. Heat 1 tbsp oil. Add jeera and dry red chillies. Let jeera turn golden.
5. Remove from fire. Add curd, stirring continuously. Return to fire. Boil. Simmer for 2 minutes on low flame and pour over the hot parwals. Serve.

Low Cal Parwals

Enjoy this low fat preparation of parwals.

Serves 4

250 gm parwals (choose green medium ones)
1 onion - sliced, ½" piece ginger - chopped
3 tbsp chopped coriander (hara dhania)

FILLING
1 large potato - boiled & mashed roughly
¾ tbsp oil
½ tsp jeera
½" piece ginger paste
1 green chilli - deseeded & chopped
¼ tsp haldi, ½ tsp red chilli powder, salt to taste
½ tsp amchoor, ½ tsp garam masala
2 tbsp chopped coriander(hara dhania)
½ tsp tomato ketchup

1. Scrape parwals and make a deep slit on a side. Scrape out the seeds by scraping the insides of the slit carefully with a knife.
2. To prepare the filling, heat ¾ tbsp oil. Add ½ tsp jeera, when it turns golden, add ginger and green chillies. Mix.
3. Remove from fire. Add 2 pinches haldi, ¼ tsp red chilli powder, ¼ tsp amchoor, ¼ tsp garam masala and ¼-½ tsp salt or to taste.
4. Return to fire. Add chopped coriander. Bhuno on low flame for 1 minute.
5. Add boiled potatoes. Stir fry for 2 minutes on low flame. Remove from fire. Add a little tomato ketchup. Mix well. Cool the filling.
6. Fill the potato mixture into the parwals. Keep aside.
7. Heat 1 tbsp oil in a pressure cooker. Add ¼ tsp jeera.
8. When jeera turns golden, add the onions and ginger. Cook till onions turn light brown.
9. Add ½ tsp salt, stuffed parwals and a lot of chopped fresh coriander. Bhuno for 2 minutes on low flame.
10. Add ¼ cup water and pressure cook to give 1 whistle. Remove from fire. After the pressure drops, bhuno a little to dry up the water.
11. To serve, cut the hot parwals into halves vertically into 2 pieces.

Tip: Parwals should never be peeled. The skin should just be scraped lightly. The green crust gives them the crunchy taste.

Moong Stuffed Tinda

Dal stuffed in round gourds.

Serves 4   *Picture on page 117*

500 gm (8-10) tinda - firm, medium sized
½ tsp salt, juice of 1 lemon, 2 tsp ginger paste
2 tsp dhania powder, ½ tsp garam masala, ¼ tsp red chilli powder, ½ tsp haldi
a few tooth picks

FILLING
75 gm (½ cup) dhuli moong dal - soaked for 2 hours
½ cup (50 gm) grated paneer
1 tbsp desi ghee or oil
a pinch of hing (asafoetida), ½ tsp jeera (cumin seeds)
1 green chilli - finely chopped, ½" piece ginger - finely chopped
½ tsp dhania powder, ½ tsp red chilli powder, ¼ tsp haldi, ¾ tsp salt, or to taste

1. Wash tindas. Scrape tindas and cut a thin slice from the top. Keep the thin slice (cap) aside. Scoop out tindas to make them hollow. Do not scoop to much.
2. Mix salt, lemon juice & ginger paste. Rub this on the inside and outside of the tindas.
3. Drain the soaked dal in a strainer.
4. Heat 1 tbsp ghee or oil in a heavy bottomed kadhai. Add a pinch of hing. Wait for 5-10 seconds.
5. Add jeera. Let jeera turn golden brown.
6. Reduce flame. Add ginger and green chilli. Mix.
7. Add dhania powder, red chilli powder and haldi.
8. Add dal. Add salt to taste and cook covered on low flame for about 8-10 minutes or till dal is done. Sprinkle a little water in-between, if it sticks to the bottom of the kadhai.
9. Add paneer and mix well. Remove from fire.
10. Stuff the dal filling inside the scooped out tindas. Press well. Cover with the cap. Secure the cap with a toothpick.
11. Heat 3 tbsp oil in a kadhai. Add ½ tsp jeera and fry till golden.
12. Reduce flame and add 2 tsp dhania powder, ½ tsp garam masala, ¼ tsp red chilli powder and ½ tsp haldi.
13. Add the stuffed tindas one by one. Gently turn them lightly, to coat the oil all over. Cover & cook on low flame for 15-20 minutes till they feel soft when a knife is inserted in them. Keep turning sides in-between to brown the tindas evenly.

Tip: When buying tindas, remember to buy ones which have very fine hair on them, are green in colour and feel firm to touch.

Hyderabadi Tindas

Whole tinda in a thick danedar masala.

Serves 4

250 gm (8-9) tinda
½ cup milk
3 tbsp oil
½ tsp jeera, a few curry leaves, ½ tsp salt, 2 tsp dhania powder
¼ tsp red chilli powder, ¼ tsp amchoor, ½ tsp garam masala
3 tbsp chopped coriander
½ cup milk

GRIND TO A PASTE
2 onions, 2 tomatoes
1 dry red or fresh green chilli, ½" piece ginger
3-4 flakes garlic - optional

FILLING
3 tbsp roasted peanuts
1 tbsp khus khus (poppy seeds), 1 tbsp til (sesame seeds)
1 tsp dhania powder, ½ tsp haldi, ¼ tsp amchoor
½ tsp salt

1. Peel and wash tindas. Give 2 cuts, crosswise in each of them but do not separate the pieces.
2. Roast separately khus khus and til on a tawa till they just change colour and become fragrant. Grind together along with peanuts to a powder.
3. To the above peanut powder, add dhania powder, haldi, chilli powder, amchoor and salt.
4. Stuff each tinda with this dry masala.
5. Heat oil in a pressure cooker, add jeera and a few curry leaves.
6. When it turns golden, add onion-tomato paste. Stir fry till dry.
7. Add ½ tsp salt, dhania powder, amchoor & garam masala. Stir fry till oil separates.
8. Add fresh coriander and mix well. Reduce heat. Add milk and cook stirring till gravy turns a little thick.
9. Add the tindas. Fry for 4-5 minutes. Add ½ cup water.
10. Pressure cook to give 1 whistle on high heat. Reduce flame and cook for another 2 minutes. Remove from fire. At serving time bhuno the tindas well so that the masala coats the tindas.

Baingan Achaari : Recipe on page 67 ➤
Hari Dahi Mein Parwal : Recipe on page 103 ➤

Lauki and Turai
(BOTTLE GOURD & RIDGE GOURD)

Rajasthani Bharwaan Lauki

Roundels of bottle gourd stuffed with paneer.

Serves 4-6　　　　*Picture on page 1*

500 gm lauki (bottle gourd) - medium thickness

FILLING
200 gm paneer - crumbled (mash roughly)
1 tsp finely chopped ginger, 1 green chilli - finely chopped
2 tbsp chopped green coriander
8-10 cashewnuts - chopped
8-10 kishmish (raisins) - soaked in water
¾ tsp salt or to taste

MASALA
2 tbsp oil or ghee
2 laung (cloves), 2 tej patta (bay leaves)
2 chhoti illaichi (green cardamoms)
1" stick dalchini (cinnamon)

TOMATO PASTE (Grind Together)
3 tomatoes
1 green chilli
½" piece ginger
½ tsp red chilli powder, 1 tsp dhania powder,¼ tsp haldi, ¾ tsp salt
½ tsp jeera (cumin seeds), ¼ tsp sugar

1. Peel lauki. Cut vertically into two pieces from the centre to get 2 smaller pieces.
2. Boil in salted water, covered, for about 10 minutes, till done. Remove from water and cool.
3. Scoop seeds from both the pieces of the lauki and make them hollow.
4. Mix paneer, green chilli, coriander, cashew nuts, kishmish and salt.
5. Stuff it into the boiled lauki pieces. Keep aside.
6. For masala- Heat ghee. Add laung, illaichi, dalchini and tej patta. Stir for a minute.
7. Add the above tomato paste. Stir for 3-4 minutes till thick and oil separates.
8. Add 1½ cups water. Boil. Simmer for 4-5 minutes till oil separates. Keep aside.
9. At serving time, saute lauki in a non stick pan in 1 tbsp oil, turning sides carefully to brown from all sides. Remove from pan.
10. Cut the lauki into ¾" thick round pieces. Transfer to a serving dish and pour the hot tomato gravy on top. Serve.

Lauki Kofta Curry

Dumplings of gourd in a light curry.

Serves 6

KOFTAS (BALLS)
1 small tender lauki (bottle gourd) (300 gm) - peeled & grated
1 boiled potato - grated
2 green chillies - deseeded & chopped
2 slices bread - sides removed & crumbled to form crumbs
1 tsp salt to taste, ½ tsp red chilli powder, ½ tsp amchoor, ½ tsp garam masala
10-12 dry aloo bukhaaras (plums) - soaked for 20 minutes & deseeded or kishmish

PASTE
2 onions
3 red tomatoes
3 green chillies
3 flakes garlic, 1" piece ginger

GRAVY
3 tbsp oil
2 laung (cloves), 1 stick dalchini (cinnamon) - broken into 2-3 pieces
½ tsp haldi, ½ tsp red chilli powder, ¼ tsp amchoor, ½ tsp garam masala
2 tsp dhania (coriander) powder
2 tbsp coriander leaves
1¼ tsp salt or to taste

1. Grate lauki finely. Squeeze it . Mix all ingredients given under the koftas in a paraat. Knead the mixture well for 4-5 minutes till well blended. Form into lemon sized balls. Insert a deseeded, soaked dry aloo-bhukhaara or a kishmish. Shape into a ball again.

2. Heat oil to deep fry the balls. Add 3-4 balls and carefully fry them on **medium flame** till they turn brown and get cooked from inside.

3. To prepare the gravy, grind together onions, tomatoes, green chillies, garlic and ginger to a paste.

4. Heat 3 tbsp oil in a kadhai and fry dalchini and laung for a few seconds.

5. Add the onion-tomato paste. Cook till dry.

6. Add all the dry masalas. Stir fry for 4-5 minutes till thick. Add 2 cups water to get a thin gravy. Boil. Add salt and coriander leaves. Simmer on low flame for 5-6 minutes. Keep aside till serving time.

7. At serving time, boil gravy. Add koftas. Give 2-3 boils and serve.

Punjabi Turai

A simple, yet tasty north Indian style.

Serves 3-4

250 gm turai (ridge gourd) - peeled & cut into thin slices
2 tbsp desi ghee or oil
¾ tsp jeera (cumin seeds)
2 onions - chopped
¼ tsp haldi
1" piece ginger - chopped
2 green chillies - deseeded and chopped
3 tomatoes - chopped
1 tsp dhania powder
½ tsp red chilli powder
½ tsp amchoor
½ tsp garam masala
1 tsp salt

1. Heat ghee in a pressure cooker. Reduce flame. Add jeera. Fry till golden brown.
2. Add onions. Fry till transparent.
3. Add haldi, ginger and green chillies. Stir fry till onions turn light brown.
4. Add tomatoes. Cook till soft and well blended with the onions.
5. Reduce flame. Add dhania powder, red chilli powder, amchoor, garam masala and salt. Cook on low flame till ghee separates.
6. Add the turai. Stir fry for 5 minutes. Add ½ cup water.
7. Close the cooker and pressure cook to give 1 whistle. Keep on low flame for 2-3 minutes. Remove from fire.
8. After the pressure drops, bhuno the turai for 2-3 minutes. Serve hot.

Saunfiyan Tori Tukri

Stuffed tori with a delicious flavour of fennel.

Picture on page 21   *Serves 3-4*

250 gm (4) tori (zuchhini) peel thinly - cut into 2" pieces to get 2-3" long pieces and give a silt lengthwise to each piece
3 tbsp oil

DRY MASALAS
½ tsp haldi
1½ tsp coriander powder
¼ tsp garam masala
¼-½ tsp red chilli powder
½ tsp amchoor
¾ tsp salt

FILLING (GRIND TOGETHER TO A PASTE WITHOUT WATER)
1 large onion
3-4 flakes garlic
½" piece ginger
1½ tsp saunf (fennel)
½ tsp salt

1. Grind together all the ingredients of filling in a grinder without water. Grind to a fine paste.
2. Add haldi, dhania powder, garam masala and red chilli powder to the prepared paste. Mix well.
3. Peel tori thinly and cut each into 2" pieces to get 2-3" long pieces. Silt each piece lengthwise.
4. Fill or stuff the tori nicely with the prepared filling. Pat the tori on top with the remaining paste.
5. Heat 3 tbsp oil in kadhai. Fry the stuffed tori in hot oil. Stir gently to mix.
6. Cover with a wet lid and cook for 8-10 minutes or till done. Stir once in between. Remove from fire and serve hot.

Other Vegetables

Sarson Ka Saag

Mustard greens - the favourite of Punjab!

Serves 6

1 bundle (1 kg) sarson ka saag (green mustard)
250 gm spinach or baathoo
2 shalgam (turnips) - peeled and chopped, optional
3-4 flakes garlic - finely chopped, optional
2" piece ginger - finely chopped
1 green chilli - chopped
¾ tsp salt, or to taste
2 tbsp makki ka atta (maize flour)
1½ tsp powdered gur (jaggery)

TADKA/TEMPERING
3 tbsp desi ghee
2 green chillies - finely chopped
1" piece ginger - finely chopped
½ tsp red chilli powder

1. Wash and clean mustard leaves. First remove the leaves and then peel the stems, starting from the lower end and chop them finely. (Peel stems the way you string green beans). The addition of stems to the saag makes it tastier but it is important to peel the stems from the lower ends. The upper tender portion may just be chopped. Wash spinach leaves. Chop the spinach or baathoo leaves and mix with sarson.
2. Put chopped greens with ½ cup water in a pan.
3. Chop garlic, ginger and green chilli very finely and add to the saag, add shalgam if you wish. Add salt and put it on fire and let it start heating.
4. The saag will start going down. Cover and let it cook on medium fire for 15-20 minutes. Remove from fire, cool.
5. Grind to a rough paste. Do not grind too much.
6. Transfer the saag to a kadhai. Add makki ka atta to the saag and cook for 15 minutes on low heat, stirring frequently. Keep aside.
7. At serving time, heat pure ghee. Reduce heat and add ginger and green chillies. Cook till ginger changes colour. Remove from fire and add red chilli powder. Add ghee to the hot saag and mix lightly. Serve hot.
8. Serve with fresh home made butter and makki-di-roti.

Note: Fresh saag should have tender leaves and tender stems (gandal).

Kathal Laajawaab

Boiled kathal (not the usual fried) coated lightly with masala.

Serves 6   *Picture on page 11*

500 gm kathal (jack fruit)
¾ tsp salt, or to taste
1 tsp dhania powder
½ tsp garam masala
¼ tsp haldi
1 tsp amchoor
½ tsp red chilli powder
5 tbsp oil
seeds of 1 moti illaichi (brown cardamom) - crushed
1 tbsp green coriander

GRIND TOGETHER TO A PASTE
1 onions - chopped roughly
2 large tomato - chopped roughly
1 green chilli
1" piece ginger
6-8 flakes garlic

1. Rub oil on your hands. Cut the whole big piece of kathal from the middle into two pieces. Remove skin. Cut widthwise from the centre of each piece. This way you get two big strips of kathal. Now further divide each strip into smaller pieces about 1" thickness, carefully to keep the shreds of the piece together . Then further divide into ½" thick pieces.

2. Boil 5 cups water with 2 tsp salt and ½ tsp haldi. Add kathal and boil uncovered for 7-8 minutes till a little soft. Keep it firm and crisp and do not over boil. Drain and keep aside.

3. Heat oil. Add onion-tomato paste and cook for 3-4 minutes. Add salt and all the masalas. Cook further for 5-7 minutes on low heat till oil separates.

4. Add the boiled kathal. Mix well gently and cook covered for 6-8 minutes on low heat till the vegetable blends well with the masala.

5. Sprinkle crushed illaichi. Mix. Serve hot garnished with chopped coriander.

Mooli Bhujia

Relish the radish greens along with the tuber.

Serves 4

4 medium sized mooli (radish) with fresh green tops
¾ tsp ajwain (carom seeds)
2 onions - finely chopped
1" piece ginger - finely chopped
1 green chilli - deseeded and chopped
1 tsp salt
1 tsp red chilli powder (optional)
¼ tsp haldi (turmeric powder)
¾ tsp garam masala
1 tsp amchoor
½ tsp sugar
4 tbsp mustard oil or any refined oil

1. Discard thick stems of leaves of 4 radish. Chop finely. Wash thoroughly in 2-3 changes of water.
2. Peel and cut only 2 radish, each into two halves lengthways. Cut each piece into thin slices. (Keep the other two radish for a salad or parantha)
3. Heat oil. Reduce flame. Add ajwain. Fry till golden brown.
4. Add chopped onion and ginger. Stir till onions turn transparent.
5. Reduce flame. Add salt, red chilli, haldi, amchoor and green chilli. Mix.
6. Now add chopped radish greens and radish pieces. Bhuno for 3-4 minutes.
7. Add sugar and garam masala. Cover and cook on low flame till radish turns tender.
8. Bhuno for 1-2 minutes. Check salt and spices. Add more if required. Serve hot.

Bathua Bhujia

Substitute radish for bathua (tops and root). Pick, clean, wash and chop bathua along with tender stems.

Phalli Tamatar aur Kairi : Recipe on page 75 ➤
Moong Stuffed Tinda : Recipe on page 105 ➤

Mixed Vegetable Jalfrezi

Crisp brown potatoes combine well with other vegetables. It is important that the potatoes be fried till golden brown and crisp.

Serves 4

2 tbsp oil
½ tsp jeera (cumin seeds)
1¼ tsp mixed seeds - ½ tsp sarson, ½ tsp kalonji, ¼ tsp methi daana
15-20 curry leaves
2 onions - cut into half rings
¼ tsp haldi

MIX TOGETHER
¾ cup tomato puree, 2 tsp tomato ketchup
2 tsp ginger-garlic paste or 2 tsp ginger-garlic - finely chopped
½ tsp red chilli powder, ½ tsp amchoor powder, 1 tsp dhania powder, 1 tsp salt

VEGETABLES
10-12 french beans - sliced diagonally into 1" pieces
1 carrot - cut diagonally into thin slices
2 potatoes - cut into fingers and fried
½ cup shelled peas - boiled
1 green capsicum - deseed and cut into thin fingers
1 long, firm tomato - cut into 4 and then cut into thin long pieces

GARNISH
1" cube of paneer

1. Boil 4 cups water with 1 tsp salt and ½ tsp sugar. Add carrots and beans after the water boils. Boil for 2 minutes till crisp-tender. Refresh in cold water.
2. Mix together - tomato puree, tomato ketchup, ginger, garlic, red chilli powder, dhania powder, amchoor and salt in a bowl. Keep aside.
3. Heat 2 tbsp oil in a kadhai. Add jeera and the mixed seeds. When jeera turns golden, reduce heat and add curry leaves and stir for a few seconds.
4. Add onions cook till golden. Add haldi. Mix.
5. Add the tomato puree mixed with dry masalas and stir on medium heat for 2 minutes.
6. Add carrot and beans. Stir for 3-4 minutes.
7. Add potatoes. Mix well.
8. Add the capsicum, peas and tomato. Stir till well blended. Remove from fire.
9. Serve garnished by finely grating paneer on the vegetables in the serving dish.

Dal & Paneer
FAVOURITES

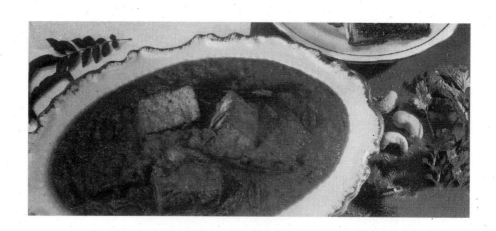

Paneer Kadhaiwaala

A semi-dry paneer preparation flavoured with coriander and fenugreek.

Serves 4-5

125 gm paneer - cut into fingers
3 large capsicums - cut into fingers
3 tbsp oil
½ tsp jeera
2 onions - cut into rings and then into halves
1 tsp ginger or garlic paste
4 tomatoes - ground to a puree in a mixer
¼ tsp haldi, 1¼ tsp salt
¼ tsp amchoor, 1 tsp dhania powder
½ tsp garam masala, ¼ tsp red chilli powder, 2 tbsp kasoori methi
¾ cup water
½ cup milk

1. Heat oil in a kadhai. Add jeera. Let it turn golden.
2. Add onions and cook till soft.
3. Add ginger or garlic paste and stir for 30 seconds.
4. Add pureed tomatoes and stir till puree turns dry.
5. Add haldi, salt, amchoor, dhania powder, garam masala, red chilli powder and kasoori methi. Stir till oil separates.
6. Add ¾ cup water mix well.
7. Add capsicum and stir for 1 minute.
8. Add paneer. Mix well gently.
9. Reduce heat and add milk, stirring continuously. Remove from fire & serve hot.

Paneer Makhani

Serves 4

250 gm paneer - cut into 1" cubes
5 large (500 gm) tomatoes - each cut into 4 pieces
2 tbsp desi ghee or butter and 2 tbsp oil
½ tsp jeera (cumin seeds)
4-5 flakes garlic and 1" piece ginger - ground to a paste (1½ tsp ginger-garlic paste)
1 tbsp kasoori methi (dried fenugreek leaves), 1 tsp tomato ketchup
2 tsp dhania powder, ½ tsp garam masala
1 tsp salt, or to taste, ½ tsp red chilli powder, preferably degi mirch
½ cup water
½-1 cup milk, approx.
½ cup cream (optional)

CASHEW PASTE
3 tbsp cashewnuts - soaked in ¼ cup warm water for 15 minutes and ground to a very fine paste

1. Boil tomatoes in ½ cup water. Simmer for 4-5 minutes on low heat till tomatoes turn soft. Remove from fire and cool. Grind the tomatoes along with the water to a smooth puree.
2. Heat oil and ghee or butter in a kadhai. Reduce heat. Add jeera. When it turns golden, add ginger-garlic paste.
3. When paste starts to change colour add the above tomato puree and cook till absolutely dry.
4. Add kasoori methi and tomato ketchup.
5. Add masalas - dhania powder, garam masala, salt and red chilli powder. Mix well for a few seconds. Cook till oil separates.
6. Add cashew paste. Mix well for 2 minutes.
7. Add water. Boil. Simmer on low heat for 4-5 minutes. Reduce heat.
8. Add the paneer cubes. Keep aside to cool till serving time.
9. At serving time, add enough milk to the cold paneer masala to get a thick curry, mix gently. (Remember to add milk only after the masala turns cold, to prevent the milk from curdling. After adding milk, heat curry on low heat.)
10. Heat on low heat, stirring continuously till just about to boil.
11. Add cream, keeping the heat very low and stirring continuously. Remove from fire immediately.
12. Garnish with 1 tbsp fresh cream, slit green chillies and coriander.

Naariyali Paneer

Coconut shreds coat paneer fingers in a dry South Indian style dish.

Serves 4-6

200 gm paneer - cut into thin fingers
4 onions - 2 grated and 2 sliced
½ cup curry leaves
6 tbsp oil
1½ tsp brown small rai (mustard seeds)
¼ of fresh coconut
1¼ tsp salt, or to taste
3 tbsp lemon juice (juice of 1 large lemon)
a pinch of tandoori red colour

RED CHILLI PASTE
4 dry, Kashmiri red chillies - deseeded and soaked in warm water for 10 minutes
1" piece ginger - chopped
1 tbsp cashews
3 tbsp curd
2 tsp dhania powder
2-3 laung (cloves), 6-7 saboot kali mirch (peppercorns)

1. Grate 2 onions. Cut the other 2 onions into halves. Then cut each half widthwise into semi-rings to get thin strips of onion.
2. Scrape the brown skin of ¼ of a coconut and grate finely to get ½ cup grated coconut.
3. Drain the soaked red chillies. Add all other ingredients of the paste and grind to a smooth paste using a little water for grinding, if required.
4. Heat oil. Add rai. Let it splutter for a minute.
5. Add grated onions and curry leaves. Cook till onions turn light brown.
6. Add onion slices and cook for 3-4 minutes till soft.
7. Add coconut and cook on low heat for 5 minutes till crisp. Keep it spread out while cooking.
8. Add red chilli paste and stir fry for 2-3 minutes.
9. Add colour and salt.
10. Add 1 cup water. Boil.
11. Add paneer and mix well.
12. Cover and cook on low heat for 5 minutes, stirring occasionally.
13. Add lemon juice and mix well. Serve hot.

Mughlai Malai Kofta

Serves 6

150 gm paneer (cottage cheese) - grated
2 small boiled potatoes - grated, 2 tbsp finely chopped poodina (mint), 2 tbsp maida
½ tsp garam masala, ¼ tsp red chilli powder, ¾ tsp salt, or to taste
2-3 tbsp maida (plain flour) - to coat

FILLING

½ onion - very finely chopped, ½" piece ginger - very finely chopped
4-5 kajus (cashews) - chopped, ¼ tsp each of salt, red chilli powder, garam masala

GRAVY

2 onion - ground to a paste
2 tbsp magaz (water melon seeds), 2 tbsp kaju - soaked in warm water, 4 tbsp curd
½ cup malai or cream - mixed with ½ cup milk
2 tbsp desi ghee or butter or 3 tbsp oil
1 tsp garam masala, ¾ tsp red chilli powder, 1 tsp kasoori methi
1 tsp salt, or to taste, 3 chhoti illaichi (green cardamoms) - crushed to a powder

GARNISH

1 tsp magaz seeds - roasted on a tawa & fresh coriander leaves

1. To prepare the koftas, mix grated paneer, potatoes, poodina, red chilli powder, salt, garam masala and 2 tbsp maida. Mix well till smooth. Make 12 balls.
3. For the filling, heat 2 tsp ghee. Add onions and ginger. Fry till golden brown. Add kaju, salt, garam masala and chilli powder. Remove from fire.
4. Flatten each ball of paneer mixture, put 1 tsp of onion filling in each ball. For a ball again. Roll each ball in a maida. Dust to remove excess maida.
5. Deep fry 1-2 koftas at a time in medium hot oil. Keep aside.
6. Soak kaju and magaz in water for 10 minutes. Drain and grind to a very fine paste with curd.
7. Heat ghee. Add grated onion. Cook on low flame till it turns transparent and ghee separates. Do not let it turn brown by keeping on high flame.
8. Add kaju – magaz paste. Cook for 2-3 minutes on low flame. Add garam masala, red chilli powder and salt.
9. Add cream. Stir. Mix well. Add kasoori methi and stir for 2 minutes.
10. Add 1½ cups water to thin down the gravy. Boil on low heat for 1 minute.
11. At the time of serving, add powdered chhoti illaichi and boil the gravy. Add koftas and simmer on low heat for 1 minute. Serve garnished with a swirl of cream, roasted magaz and fresh coriander leaves.

Note: If the koftas break on frying, roll them in cornflour and then fry.

Paneer & Vegetable Korma

Korma is a gravy prepared with curd, cashew paste and sometimes even coconut.

Serves 4

150 gm paneer - cut into 1" cubes and fried till golden

½ cup shelled peas - boiled or frozen

1 small slice of tinned pineapple - cut into 1" pieces, optional (see note)
1-2 small carrots - cut into thin round slices
4 tbsp oil, 3-4 laung (cloves), 1" stick dalchini (cinnamon)
2 onions - cut into slices
¼ tsp haldi (turmeric) powder, 1 tsp dhania powder
½ tsp garam masala
1½ tsp salt
1-1½ cups milk

GRIND TOGETHER (CASHEW-CURD PASTE)
2 tbsp til (sesame seeds) & 3 tbsp cashews - soaked in warm water for 10 minutes and drained
¾ cup curd
2 tsp grated coconut (fresh or desiccated), optional
1½" piece ginger
6-8 flakes garlic
seeds of 2-3 chhoti illaichi (green cardamom)

1. Soak til and cashews. Drain. Grind them with coconut, ginger, garlic and chhoti illaichi together to a paste alongwith curd.
2. Heat oil. Add laung and dalchini. Wait for a minute. Add onions. Cook till onions turn golden brown.
3. Add haldi and dhania powder, garam masala and salt. Stir to mix well for a minute on low heat.
4. Reduce heat. Add the cashew-curd paste. Cook on low heat till oil separates.
5. Add carrots. Stir for 2 minutes.
6. Add 1 cup water or enough to get a thick gravy. Boil. Simmer covered for 8-10 minutes or more till the carrots get done.
7. Add peas, paneer and pineapple. Boil for 1 minute.
8. Reduce heat. Add milk on low heat, stirring continuously. Add enough milk to get the desired consistency of the gravy. Serve sprinkled with garam masala and chopped coriander.

Note: The left over pineapple can be stored in a steel box in the freezer compartment of the refrigerator without getting spoilt.

Dal Makhani

The simplest, yet the tastiest recipe of the all time favourite dal.

Serves 4-6

PRESSURE COOK TOGETHER
1 cup kali daal (urad saboot) - soaked for 4-5 hours
2 dry red chillies
1 tbsp desi ghee or butter
2 tsp ginger-garlic paste

OTHER INGREDIENTS
500 (5 large) tomatoes - grind to a puree
1 tbsp kasoori methi
1 tsp ginger-garlic paste
2-3 tbsp butter
1 tsp tomato ketchup
2 tsp dhania powder
½ tsp garam masala
1½ tsp salt, or to taste
¼ tsp grated nutmeg (jaiphal)
1 tsp tandoori masala, optional
1 cup milk
¼- ½ cup cream, optional

1. Drain the water from the dal. Pressure cook dal with 5 cups fresh water, red chillies, desi ghee or butter and ginger-garlic paste. After the first whistle keep on low heat for 40 minutes.
2. Remove from fire and let the pressure drop by itself.
3. Remove the whole dried chillies from the cooked dal.
4. Put the dal back on fire. Add freshly pureed tomatoes, kasoori methi, 1 tsp ginger-garlic paste, butter, tomato ketchup, dhania and garam masala.
5. Cook for about 20 minutes, mashing the dal till a thick, smooth dal is ready.
6. Add milk and tandoori masala. Cook further for 5-7 minutes till you get the right colour.
7. Reduce heat and add cream and jaiphal. Remove from fire and serve hot.

Note: If cream is not to be added, add a little extra milk.

Dal Dakshini

Yellow dal with a South Indian tempering.

Serves 4

¾ cup arhar ki dal
¼ cup channe ki dal
½ tsp haldi
1½ tsp salt

TADKA
3 tbsp oil or ghee
1 tsp jeera, 1 tsp sarson
3-4 tbsp curry leaves
1-2 dry, red chillies
1 onion - chopped finely
1 tsp fresh ginger paste
1 tomato - pureed in a mixer
1 tomato - chopped finely
1 tsp dhania powder
½ tsp garam masala
¼ tsp red chilli powder
1 tbsp imli pulp or juice of ½ lemon, or to taste
some chopped coriander

1. Clean, wash dals. Add haldi, salt and 3 cups of water. Pressure cook to give 1 whistle. Keep on low flame for 5 minutes. Remove from fire.
2. For the tadka, heat oil or ghee. Add jeera and sarson. Let jeera turn golden.
3. Add curry leaves and dry red chillies.
4. Add onion and cook till light golden. Add ginger paste. Stir for a minute.
5. Add freshly pureed tomatoes. Cook till tomato turns dry.
6. Add chopped tomato and cook for 2-3 minutes till soft.
7. Add masalas – dhania powder, garam masala and red chilli powder. Stir for 2 minutes on low heat.
8. Add imli pulp or juice of ½ lemon. Mix well and pour on the cooked dal. Mix lightly and serve sprinkled with some coriander.

Khoya Matar Makhaana : Recipe on page 24 ➤
Safed Jalpari : Recipe on page 96 ➤

Nita Mehta's BEST SELLERS

Delicious Parlour ICE CREAMS

DESSERTS & PUDDINGS

CAKES & CHOCOLATES

Food for Children

Different ways with CHAAWAL

The Art of BAKING

JHATPAT KHAANA

Indian Cooking Handi Tawa Kadhai

(AWARD WINNER)

STAY SLIM...EAT RIGHT

Flavours of INDIAN COOKING (All Colour)

PRESSURE COOKING

LOW FAT Tasty Recipes

Dal & Roti

PASTA & CORN

SOUTH INDIAN Favourites

Taste of GUJARAT

Mocktails & Snacks

NAVRATRI RECIPES

Green Vegetables

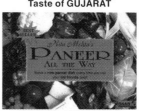
PANEER All The Way

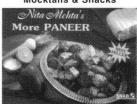
MORE PANEER

Eggless OVEN Recipes

BREAKFAST Non-Vegetarian

PARTY FOOD

CHINESE Non-Vegetarian